CRICUT

EXPLORE AIR 2

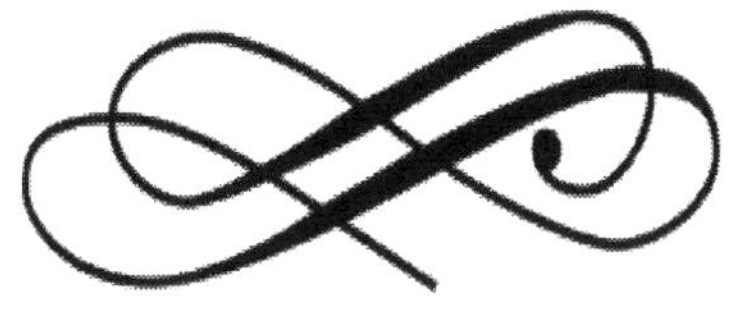

Amanda Vinyl

Table of Contents

Introduction

Cricut Explore Air 2 is a small die cutting machine designed to reduce at twice the speed of Cricut Explore Air, its earliest version. One unique thing about Cricut Explore Air 2 is that its tools are made of high quality and has two cutting modes: fast and normal modes, to deliver your project with precision.

There are many materials this machine can cut, including paper, cardstock, iron-on, fabric, poster board, washi sheet, faux leather, aluminum foil, felt, vellum, magnetic cloth, canvas, and more. I do not intend to dwell much on this machine because there are many works of literature you can use to get yourself familiarized with the technology, but brief pros and cons are given below.

Pros and Cons

I am particularly pleased with Cricut Explore Air 2 because it is compatible with smart devices, including smartphones, tablets, and computers. Use any of these devices to design beautiful crafts that you can print then cut by Cricut Explore Air 2 machine. You even have the flexibility of starting a design on one of your devices and finishing on another device. The good thing about this feature is that every minute will count for you in your project, whether you are on the bus, taxi, metro, or anywhere you can use your device comfortably.

There are 3000+ easy-to-use projects pre-designed in the library, and Cricut Explore Air 2 can use this extensive image library, so you don't need to be a professional to make use of the Cricut Explore Air 2 machine to realize beautiful and super unique crafts that you have always desired to produce.

The Bluetooth enabled device gives you the freedom to send designs directly from another Bluetooth let instrument, including your phone, thereby eliminating the need for an adapter. The speed at which this machine performs the cutting and writing operation is its main selling point. It has both standard and fast modes of operation.

Other pros for this exciting crafter's companion, Cricut Explore Air 2 include the fact that it comes in excellent and stunning colors like the one with the green color shown in the diagram below, accessible storage compartments, and the powerful cutting blades for different materials, including wood and leather.

Like every manufactured device, Cricut Explore Air 2 has its cons. One drawback of the Cricut Explore Air 2 machine from the other cutters is that it is only compatible with the web-based Design Space software. This means that you need internet connectivity before working with this software to design those super unique projects. The software is compelling and can be used by professionals and beginners.

Another drawback is the high noise level compared to other Cricut machines. This is expected because it is designed to cut with more power, in fact, the strength of its cut and speed of amount is twice that of Cricut Explore Air.

Even with these disadvantages, Cricut Explore Air 2 is a fantastic cutting machine that will give you massive value for money.

CHAPTER 1:

What is Cricut?

Overview

The Cricut Explore Air is a die-cutting system (aka craft plotter or cutting-edge system). You can consider it such as a printer; you also make an image or layout in your personal computer and then ship it to your device. Except that Rather than printing your design, the Cricut machine cuts out of whatever substance you desire! The Cricut research air can reduce paper, vinyl, cloth, craft foam, decal paper, faux leather, and longer!

In reality, if you would like to utilize a Cricut just like a printer, then it may do this also! There's an attachment slot on your system, and you're able to load a mark in there, after which possess the Cricut "draw" the layout for you. It is ideal for obtaining a stunning handwritten look if your design is not all that good.

The Cricut explore air may reduce stuff around 12" broad and includes a little cutting blade mounted within the system. When you are prepared to cut out something, you load the things on a sticky mat and then load the mat to your machine. The mat holds the material in place while the Cricut blade moves over the substance and cuts. If it finishes, then you unload the carpet in the machine, then peel off your project the mat, and then you are all set to move!

Using a Cricut system, the options are infinite! All you want is a Cricut system, design space, something to reduce, along with your creativity!

What Could I Do with a Cricut Machine?

There are a lot of things you can perform using a Cricut device! There is no way that I could list all of the possibilities, however, here are a couple of popular kinds of jobs to provide you a good concept about exactly what the machine could perform.

- Cut out interesting shapes and letters to get cartoons
- Make a habit, handmade cards for any specific event (here is an illustration)
- Layout an onesie or some t-shirt (here is an illustration)
- Create a leather necklace
- Create buntings and other party decorations
- Make your stencils for painting (here is an illustration)
- Create a plastic decal for your vehicle window
- Tag material on your cabinet or in a playroom
- Make monogram cushions
- Make your own Christmas decorations (here is an illustration)
- Address an envelope
- Decorate a mug cup, or tumbler (here is an illustration)
- Etch glass at house (here is an illustration)
- Make your wall stickers

- Create a painted wooden signal
- Create your own window
- Cut appliqués or quilt squares
- Produce stickers to get a rack mixer

...and plenty of different jobs, which are too many to list!

Unboxing the Cricut Explore Air 2 Machine

After purchasing the Cricut Explore Air 2 machine, it is essential to make sure it has all its accessories wholly boxed in, and nothing is missing. If you find anything missing, you are advised to return it to where it was purchased or simply contact Cricut support and inform them about the missing accessories. A complete packaged Cricut Explore Air 2 machine should have the following items in it:

- Cricut Explore Air 2
- Instruction manual
- Cricut cutting mat
- Cutting blade
- Silver pen and the accessory adapter
- Power and the USB cords
- The Cardstock and the Vinyl samples

It is to be noted that we have different kinds available, and depending on the kits you purchased, your Cricut Explore Air 2 machine might come with extra items included in it. The following are different kinds of packages available for the Cricut Explore Air 2 machine:

- Ultimate Kit
- Tools Kit
- Vinyl starter Kit
- Complete Starter Kit
- The Premium Vinyl

Different Parts of the Cricut Explore Air 2

Cutting Mat

The Cutting Mat gives a platform on how the materials are going to be laid into the Cricut Machine. It helps in getting the material securely placed by being sticky, holds on firmly to the material.

Tool Cup

The tool cup is the part that holds scissors, pens, and other Cricut tools in use. The pen is used by getting the accessory clamp A opened and dropping in the pen down into it, after which the clamp is then closed.

Accessory Storage Compartments

Apart from the Tool Cup, the Cricut Explore Air 2 machine is made up of two compartments, which are also used in holding tools. These are:

- Smaller Compartment
- Larger Compartment

The smaller compartment is positioned at the left for holding additional blade housings, the accessory adapter, and the blades. The smaller chamber is made up of a magnetic strip for securely keeping the replacement blades and prevents them from rolling.

The larger compartment is used to store longer tools and pens.

Accessory Clamp A

The accessory clamp A comes pre-installed as the accessory adapter, and the pen for drawing instead of having to cut can be inserted through this part. It also helps in holding the scoring blades.

Blade Clamp A

Cricut Explore Air Machine has the Blade clamp A already pre-installed in them. The replacement or the removal of bits of vinyl can also be done here.

Smart Set Dial

The Cricut Explore Air machine, through its fast mode of operation, enables the user to turn and indicate which material is to be cut with the twice fast mode with the use of the Smart Set dial. All you need to do is to rotate the Smart Set dial and choose the material you will be cutting.

Removing and Replacing the Accessory and the Blade clamps of the Cricut Explore Air Machine

To remove the accessory clamp or blade, pull open the lever, after which you will then get the metal housing pulled out.

The blade is positioned seated inside; having a tiny plunger on the top, pressing this down, will reveal the blade held magnetically.

To get the blade replaced, if the need arises, all you have to do is to get the blade pulled out and drop the new blade in.

Features of the Cricut Explore Air 2 Machine

- The Cricut Explore Air 2 machine is a wireless design and cut system kind of device.
- It can cut different varieties of materials easily because it has the Smart set dial.
- Cricut Explore Air 2 machine is a fast mode machine that enables it to cut and write twice as fast according to the tools and the images you are cutting.
- To make effective use of the Fast Mode, you are advised to select the Fast Mode in the design space and set the material between Vinyl and Cardstock.
- Accessories such as the blade, blade housing, and the accessory adapter are all pre-installed in the Cricut Explore Air 2 machine.
- You will find settings of most common materials displayed on the dial, and there is an entire library of materials present in the Design space. You are advised to set the dial to custom.
- The Cricut Explore Air 2 machine has adequate storage, which makes everything you need readily available in it.
- The Cricut Explore Air 2 machine is an automated machine that enables it to adjust the Smart Set dials for the user.
- It also has a cup that helps in holding your tools and has two accessory compartments, the small and large compartments.
- The smaller compartment has magnetic strips that help in holding additional housings and the accessory adapter.

The larger compartment helps in the storage of different Cricut tools.

The Cricut Explore Air 2 machine is made up of cartridge ports. The cartridge helps in linking your cartridges to your Cricut account online, which, in turn, helps you to access your

Useful Tips

Once you go through this process of getting your machine setup, the machine will be registered automatically.

In a situation where you couldn't go through with the setup when the Cricut was connected to your PC at first, you will need to get the machine reconnected and visit the design portal on the Cricut website, or visit the Design Space Account menu, select New Machine Setup and follow the on-screen instructions that come up.

How to Set Up Your Cricut Machine

The Explore Air 2 is compatible with Smart devices such as Tablets, Smartphones, and Pcs. This is a very helpful feature. For example, you can create a design while in transit and click print when you get home.

Now you just purchased the Cricut Explore Air 2 machine, confused on how to set it up?

Follow these easy steps to set up your Explore Air 2;

For iOS/Android

- After you must have plugged your machine in, switch it on, pair your device with the Cricut machine via Bluetooth.
- Download and install the Design space.
- Launch the app, sign in, or create a Cricut ID.

- Tap Menu and select "machine setup" and "App overview."
- Select new machine set up
- Follow on-screen instructions to complete the setup.

To set up this Cricut Explore Machine, here are some of the steps to follow.

- Plug in the machine and turn it on.
- Enter your browser, go to
- DesignCricut.Com/Setup.
- Follow the instructions on the screen to sign-up or create your Cricut ID and press submit.
- Download and install the design or software. You will be asked to make your first project to know that your setup is complete.
- You will need to set up your machine with your personal computer and perform your first project on the Cricut.

It is recommended to know the exact spot to place your machine before proceeding to set up the machine. It is more recommended to put your machine near your computer or where you will be using another connected device such as a tablet.

Even though the Cricut cutter can operate wirelessly without connecting directly to a computer, it is ideal for you to be near the machine for easy access to load and unload mats and pressing the necessary buttons.

You should also consider which perfect surface to place the machine on—a flat surface with 10 inches from the machine will be a great choice to guide against unloading mats falling on the floor or hanging awkwardly.

You will need a range of 10 inches of space above the top of your machine. This space creates a room to open the machine's lid and easily put in things like the pen into the Cricut machine.

The following steps will show you how to set up your machine correctly:

- Plugin your machine to the power source with the power adaptor and switch it on.
- Connect your Cricut explore machine to the computer using the USB cable.
- Open the web browser on your computer and log on to the Cricut website. Login if you already have a Cricut account, but if you are new, go-ahead to set up a Cricut account on the website.
- After creating your account, you are now ready to set up your Cricut machine by connecting to the Cricut website's design portal.
- Click on the download icon to download the latest plugin software.
- After implementing the above process, the below steps will guide you through the completion of the installation process, either you are a Mac or a PC user.

For Windows/Mac

- After downloading the software, click and open the Finder in the Mac toolbar.

- The next step is to locate the downloaded folder on your computer and double-click the Cricut Design Space file you already downloaded.
- The terms and conditions will come up, review, and agree to it.
- Drag to the right the np—Cricut plugin into the Internet Plugin folder.
- After this, click the authenticate icon.
- After you have authenticated the Internet Plugins, close the Cricut Design Space and download the windows frame to return to your Mac browser.
- Discontinue your browser and return to the Cricut website to continue with the setup process.
- Click on the "Detect Machine" icon and click continue when your Cricut machine has been detected.
- If you do not want to subscribe to the software, check the box to enable your trial subscription, and tap continue.
- After this, you will receive a thank you note denoting that your Cricut Explore Air 2 is all set up for your first cutting project.
- Hint to take full advantage of the free trial subscription; do make sure you check the open trial box before you click continue. This page comes up for both the Mac and PC installation process.
- Also, your free trial subscriptions allow you to access the Cricut image library of over 30,000 images and 300 fonts without a credit card or any other requirements needed.

Installation for PC

- After downloading the Plugin software to your PC, close your browser.
- Tap the start menu and click to open the documents folder.
- Select downloads and double click the Cricut Design Space file to open the setup of the file.
- Then click continue when the setup is on.
- Review the terms and conditions and click the accept button.
- Follow the instructions to install the software.
- When you have successfully installed the Cricut Design Space software, click the finish button.
- Next is to tap on the "Detect Machine" icon, when your machine has been detected, tap "continue."
- Check the box to access the free trial subscription, and then click continue.
- You will also get the thank you card to ascertain that your Cricut Machine is set up and that you are ready to carry out your first cut.

How to Cut Heavyweight and Lightweight Materials

Calibration makes it easy for you to use a blade when you want to use it for the first time. You must complete the calibration because it helps the Cricut machine recognize the type of blade housing you wish to use. The calibration is done in the blade housing that contains the blade. So anytime you feel like replacing a blade, you don't need to calibrate the machine again because it has already been calibrated. The only reason you should recalibrate the blade housing is if you want to use a different blade housing in the machine. Otherwise, there will be no need for recalibration.

How to Calibrate Your Cricut Air 2

We will be starting with how to calibrate the knife blade before forging ahead on other calibration.

Put a white piece of printing paper on the cutting mat. Align it and select continue.

A menu will drop down. Select the machine in use.

An option will tell you to insert your mat with the printed paper into the machine with the load/unload button. Select load.

After you are done, select "Go" to begin calibration.

Your Cricut Explore Air 2 will cut seven sets of lines that overlap in the middle. Remove the mat from the machine. With caution, determine which cut has the best overlap.

The best cuts usually appear as a single cut. Once you have made your selection, select "Continue" from the drop-down menu.

How to Calibrate Your Printer for Print Then Cut

Print then Cut is a feature that's found in the Cricut Design Space. Calibrating your printer will allow it to print and then cut the image with better precision. Without print then cut calibration, your Cricut Explore will not exactly cut your printed images well.

If you must be using the Print, then Cut feature on your Cricut Explore Air 2 for the first time, you will have to calibrate it. Most Cricut Explore

Air 2 comes pre-calibrated. However, if yours did not come calibrated, follow the steps below to set up your Print then Cut calibration.

Select "Calibration" from the Account drop-down menu. Ensure you have signed in with the correct details.

You will see "Start Calibration" with a note and a green button with "Continue" by the end of the right-hand side of the screen. Select the green button.

Load any measurement of a white paper material into your printer as a calibration sheet. Don't load colored materials as it will hinder your Cricut from reading the cut sensor or marks correctly.

Click “Continue.”

A print dialogue box will appear. Confirm if the destination is your printer and click “Print.”

Now, connect your Cricut Explore Air 2 to a computer. You can use either Mac or Windows. Ensure your Cricut is powered on.

Once the Explore Air 2 has been detected, place the calibration sheet on the cutting mat. Follow the instructions on the screen carefully.

Load the calibration sheet into your Cricut Explore Air 2 and turn the smart set dial to the paper setting.

Select “Go” on your Cricut.

You will see the cut sensor marks around your images. Make a test cut around the little center square in the middle.

Once it is done cutting, observe the nature of the cutting. Notice the small cut lines around the small square at the center. If the cut lines similarly went around the printed line, select "Yes" and then "Continue."

Your Cricut Explore Air 2 will make some vertical and some horizontal cuts on the calibration sheet. When your Cricut is done cutting, observe again the lines around the print page. Which cuts are closest to the print line?

After you have selected the corresponding numbers in the menu, select "Continue."

Your Cricut will cut the bigger rectangle. When it is done cutting, observe the precision of the cut line. If satisfactory, select "Yes," followed by "Continue." Otherwise, select "No" and then "Continue."

Select "Save and close."

How to Calibrate a Rotary Blade

Each time you change a rotary blade, you must perform a rotary blade calibration to enhance precise cutting. It is worthy to note that the Cricut rotary blade is exclusive to the Cricut maker only. That's because the Cricut Explore Air 2 lacks an Adaptive Tool System to control how the blade is used. However, we are talking about Cricut calibration so, it is fair we talk about rotary blade calibration for users that have other Cricut machines.

Calibrating the rotary blade is simple and similar to that of a knife blade. To calibrate the rotary blade:

Click open Design Space on your Mac/Windows PC.

Select "Menu" and click "Calibration." You must have inserted your rotary blade housing. Remember to insert your knife blade into clamp "B."

Select "Rotary blade" among the three calibration options.

Put a white piece of printing paper on the cutting mat. Align it and select continue.

A menu will dropdown. Select the machine in use.

An option will tell you to insert your mat with the printed paper into the machine with the load/unload button. Select load.

After you have done so, select “Go” to begin calibration.

Congratulations! Your knife blade calibration is complete.

A rotary blade can cut the following fabrics without any hindrance;

- Canvas
- Cashmere
- Cotton
- Faux leather
- Fleece
- Linen
- Velvet
- Silk
- Polyester, etc.

How to Design with Cricut Machine

Cricut Design Space is Cricut’s software program that is used to create design files the Cricut machine understands. In other words, it is a web-based program that lets you browse through pages of your projects, including your created designs on your phone, laptop, etc. It also allows you to upload your fonts and image files in jpeg format.

Before you use the Cricut Design Space, you will need to create an account. This account will grant you access to your saved projects, designs, and your personal information. We will show you how to get Cricut Explore Air 2 set up on your computer.

How to Create an Account

To create an account on Cricut Design Space;

1. Log in to https://design.Cricut.com/.
2. Select the "Get Started" green box at the lower end of the page.
3. A fill-in form tab will open on the next page, fill in your first name, last name, email address, country, and password. Three countries will appear when you select "country," United States, Canada, and the United Kingdom.
4. Read the terms before ticking the "I accept the Cricut Terms of Use" box.
5. If you want the Cricut tutorials, inspiration, and deals to be sent to you periodically via email, consider checking the box.
6. Click on "Create User ID."
7. A confirmation page will open in the next window, citing that your account has been created.
8. Cricut might want to know you better by asking you a few questions. Select "Continue" and fill in the most accurate answers.
9. Download and Install the Cricut Design Space program.

10. Another window will pop up, with a setup wizard taking you through all the processes of setting up your program.

11. Read and accept the terms of the agreement.

12. Cricut Design Space plugin will begin installing on your computer.

Your account should have been created by now, and the installation of the software should have been completed.

Working with Fonts in the Design Space

Cricut Design Space permits the use of fonts downloaded from third party sites. That means if you don't want to use the custom fonts in the Cricut Design Space, you can download the fonts on your Windows/Mac system through the Chrome browser.

How to Add Text to Cricut Design Space

1. For Windows users, navigate to the left-hand side of the Canvas and select the Text tool. For iOS or Android user, the Text tool is at the bottom-left of the screen.

2. Select the font size and the font type you wish to use and then type your text in the text box. Do not freak out when you did not choose the font parameters before typing the text. With Cricut Design Space, you can type the text before selecting the font on Windows/Mac computer.

3. Click or tap on any space outside the text box to close it.

How to Edit Text in Cricut Design Space

To edit the text is super simple. Double click on the text to show available options. Select the action you wish from the list of the options displayed, including font style, type, size, letter, and line spacing.

How to Edit Fonts

If Cricut doesn't have your desired font, follow these steps below:

1. First of all, download a font. If you are using a Windows or Mac system, use a Google Chrome browser to download because it works pretty great with Cricut Design Space.

2. Ensure you know the exact location of the folder where your font is downloaded. Click to open the downloaded font. You may need to extract the font using extraction software if there is a need to.

3. Double click on the font file. Once you have done this, a tab will open for installation. Click install.

Congratulations, your font is installed in your Cricut Design Space. Remember always to refresh Design Space to show your installed font.

How to Write Using System Fonts

System fonts refer to fonts installed on your computer or mobile device. Every time you sign in, the Cricut Design Space will automatically access your system fonts and allow you to use them for free in the Design Space projects.

Some system fonts have design components that are not compatible with Cricut Design space because they were not designed by Cricut. Do not be surprised when you encounter failure to import them into the Design Space or behave unusually while using them in the Design Space.

Use the instructions on the font size or app when downloading fonts to your device or computer.

Using a font in Cricut Design Space isn't as difficult as it seems if you know how to use it. The following steps will explain in details how to use a font in a Cricut Design Space:

1. After you must have installed your font, restart your Cricut Design Space to refresh all the fonts, including your new font.

2. In the work area of your Cricut Design Space, click, "Text" icon to start writing your text.

3. Add your text. Ensure the text is highlighted.

4. Click on "Font."

5. From the drop-down on the taskbar, select "System Fonts." All your fonts in the system will load at once. This may take a few seconds.

6. Select your preferred font.

7. The selected or highlighted text will be displayed in the new font.

That's it. Your text is now in your new font.

How to Use Images in Cricut Design Space

Despite the large library of custom images the Cricut Design Space has, there are files that you may want to cut yourself that may not be available in the system. Since Cricut Design Space supports DIY designs, you can design your own files and upload them to the Design Space for cutting. You can either use Adobe Illustrator or Photoshop to create your own designs.

There are two types of images you can upload, basic images and vector images. Cricut Design Space supports both file types. The uploads are different, but the result is the same. Basic images such as JPG and PNG are uploaded as a single layer. In contrast, vector images like SVG are separated into layers. It is the same process you use for uploading a vector file and a basic file.

How to Cut One Image Out of Another Image

It is possible to remove a part of an image to form another image using the Slice tool in Design Space and is super easy. Use these steps to remove an image out of another image:

1. Position the two images to overlap each other.
2. Select the two images.
3. Click on "Slice." This button is at the bottom of the Layers Panel for computer users, in the Actions menu at the bottom of the screen for Android and iOS users.
4. Separate the layers to review your new shapes.
5. Edit or delete the images separately.
6. Go to Layer and slice your image till you get your desired design.

How to Upload Images on Cricut Design Space

Uploading your images to Design Space is a walk in the park once you grasp the basic concepts. As stated earlier, there are two significant categories of image files that can be uploaded to the Design Space.

Vector Images; .dxf and .svg files. They are uploaded in more than one layer in such a way that you can edit varying independent parts on the platform.

Basic Images; .png, .jp, .gif and .bmp are uploaded in the form of a single-layered image. This implies that what you see in the preview of the image before printing and cutting is exactly what you will get after the whole process is completed.

After your image is ready, which you might have bought on the Cricut platform or designed yourself, it is time to upload it. The next logical step to take is to open the Design Space.

Open a new project and tap on the Upload Image icon at the screen's top left-hand side.

Tap on the 'Browse Files" tab and search for the relevant file from your PC.

If the file is a vector image, a preview will come up after the upload is complete. At this point, you can rename the image and save it from this point.

On the other hand, if the file is a basic image, you can carry out any of the following functions;

- Select the type of image; this serves to determine the complexity of the image. If the image been uploaded does not contain too much information, you can pick the Simple Image option, and if the details in the image are much, you can select the Moderately or Complex Image Options.

- Tap on the Continue icon.

- Select and Erase; here, you can carry out the editing process on your basic image. This involves erasing and cropping out the unneeded parts by making use of the available tools. When you are satisfied with the result, tap on the continue button.

- Name and Tag; in this section, you can give your image a name and decide if it will be a cut image or a print and cut image.
- Save
- You will then be taken back to the upload image screen.
- Pick the image and click on the Insert Image button located on the bottom left corner of the screen.

The image is now prepared and ready to be cut or printed.

How to Clean the Cricut Machine

Cleaning your Cricut machine involves basically caring for your mat. All other cleanings will have to do with the maintenance of your machine.

There are different ways of cleaning the Cricut mat based on their types:

For Fabricgrip Cricut Mat

1. Do not use the scraper tool to remove bits of fabric on the Cricut mat, unlike other Cricut mats
2. The oils on your finger can reduce the adhesive on the mat's surface, so avoid touching the surface with your fingers.
3. Use only Cricut spatula, tweezers, or StronGrip transfer tape to clean this mat.
4. Cleaning agents including soap and water should not be used on this mat

For Other Mats

1. Use the tool called scrapper to clear all the leftovers from your Cricut mat

2. For smaller leftover bits difficult to remove, use a sticky lint roller and roll it over your Cricut mat to remove them.

3. Wash your Cricut mat with any gentle detergent and water and allow it to dry.

4. Use a nonalcoholic cleaning wipe to clean the surface of your Cricut mat.

FAQS About The Cricut Explore Air

Where Can I Download Software for My Cricut Explore Air Machine?

For iOS users or Android users, you can get Cricut Design Space on the iOS App Store and Google Play, respectively. All you need do is to download it, install it, and log in

For uses on a computer, visit design.cricut.com and then sign in with your login details. There will be a prompt to download Cricut Design Space. Download the plugin and install it, and you are good to go.

Does My Cricut Explore Air Need a Wireless Bluetooth Adapter?

No. Your machine is Bluetooth enabled. There is no need for a wireless Bluetooth adapter.

Can I Link My Cartridges to More Than One Account?

No. You can link your cartridges to only one Cricut account.

Can a Cartridge Be Unlinked After It Has Been Linked?

No. A cartridge once linked to an account cannot be unlinked.

I Linked My Cartridge to Older Software; Can I Still Use It in Cricut Design Space?

Once you have linked your cartridges to older software like Cricut Craft Room, there will be no need to relink them on Cricut Design Space because they will be automatically available there.

I Have Linked My Cartridges; How Do I Access Them?

All the cartridges you have linked to your account can be found in your Cricut account. Go to Cricut Design Space and look under "My Image Sets" in the Insert Images window. You will find all the cartridges you have linked to your account.

Can I Use Physical Cartridges Without Linking Them?

No. To use any cartridge on your Cricut Explore Air, it must be linked to your account.

What Type of Materials Can I Cut with My Cricut

This machine cut more than 80 types of materials, clipboard, soda cans, and even thicker materials.

Can I Upload My Own Images?

Yes, you can upload your image or any other files that are already formatted and are compatible with Cricut design space? The SVGs is one of the best image files because it uses 37 math formulas to create images based on points between lines.

What is the Duration of My Cutting Mat?

You can cut through each cutting mat 20-50 full cut, but it depends on the card stack's nature and the cut size?

Can I Make Use of Other Paper Sizes?

Yes, you can. One corner of the paper can just be lined up with the mat before loading your mat. Use the blade navigation button to adjust the cutting blade to the upper right side of the paper.

After which you tap on set paper size on your keypad, then allow the machine to start cutting on your paper

Can I Learn How to Create My Own Customize Project with Cricut Design Software Without Much Stress?

You can create and design your custom project any way you wish it to be without much weight.

Do I Need a Cricut?

Cricut machine is a dream come true for decorators and crafters. It has innumerable applications like card making, paper flower, labeling, leather key chain, you name it! Cricut machine is ideal and is a relief for you if you do crafting, which requires a lot of cutting. Only then you can get the total benefit of this amazing machine. However, if crafting is just a normal hobby that you do once a year, then the Cricut machine is not for you.

Are There Other Devices That Can Do the Same Thing?

Yes, there are many options. Some devices can exactly do the work which the Cricut machine is doing.

Is Cricut Better Than the Rest of the Machines Out There?

I believe every machine that cuts materials and eases crafting is amazing. But to pick the best one, you can go through the reviews on Amazon, which Cricut has between four to five stars. Pretty great!

Why Should I Prefer Cricut Over Other Crafting Machines?

Simple, because it is the one you want. You will get mixed reviews for Cricut; you will hate it, and others are its die-hard fan. But in the end, it's you who has to pay from your pocket for your choice. So choose that machine with which you are comfortable. Also, check for the tools and accessories, and make sure that whatever you are planning to purchase, makes crafting easier and enjoyable for you. Another thing about Cricut is that it is much more than a machine; it's actually a community. There are tons of free tutorials to get you to get started with Cricut and ideas to proficient your skills. And fellow creatives love to share their tips and tricks of this super fantastic tool.

What Are the Available Machines Out There?

Right now, there are three models of Cricut machines.

1 - Cricut Explore Family: These are the most common Cricut machines and comes with three different machines based on their features.

- Cricut Explore – 1: The firstborn of the Cricut Explore family that only has one tool holder for drawing and cutting separately.

- Cricut Explore Air: It also has Bluetooth, so it's a blessing for the crafter who hates cords.

- Cricut Explore Air – 2: Have features of previous products, but it's two times faster.

2 - Cricut Maker: This is the latest release and great for cutting thick materials like wood and leather.

3 - Cricut Cuttlebug: This Cricut machine comes with the added feature of embossing on the substrate. But this machine doesn't have access to Design space or the internet. However, it is a powerful cutter.

There are other machines available on Amazon, but they are not compatible with Cricut Design Space. So, don't buy any old version of Cricut.

Is the Cricut Machine Expensive?

Yes, purchasing a Cricut machine is quite expensive. However, it is a one-time investment and comes with good deals. And you can start with your crafting projects right away with it.

Is It Worth My Money?

That depends on your priorities, hobbies, and budget. Like I said before, if you are a seasonal crafter, then the Cricut machine doesn't worth your money. Weight its pros and cons and then make a decision.

Just ask this question if you are thinking of buying a Cricut machine. Is Cricut going to make your life easier and enjoyable? Does it save time?

Because time is money.

If yes, then buy the Cricut.

What is the Best Cricut Machine for Me?

If the Cricut meets the following requirements, then it is the best for you:

1- It is affordable

2- It can cut the materials you want

3- It will save money for you to buy materials

If all three options are checked, then you should buy Cricut Air Explore 2. It's affordable than other Cricut machines. If you only want to cut fabric, paper, and vinyl, then Cricut can do this job much better. Last but not least, there is no point in buying an expensive Cricut if it doesn't leave you a spare for you to buy additional materials.

Should I Upgrade My Cricut Machine?

Congrats on buying and working with Cricut. It's rocking, isn't it?

So are you now considering upgrading it? You may feel it because now most of the tutorials are for the Cricut Maker, and you may think it's time for an update.

Not at all. Treat your Cricut machine like your cell phone or car. Do you upgrade it every year? Unless you do and have a budget, you can surely upgrade Cricut to the newest version.

Where Can I Shop for Cricut?

You can get Cricut from many places. Amazon, Walmart Store, and many craft stores keep it. Even Cricut's own website offers the best deals and bundles for shopping Cricut. If you want to purchase Cricut right now, head over to its official website.

Where Can I Find Cricut and its Materials on Sale?

Answer: You can find Cricut and the materials on sale easily. In fact, the sale is on pretty much all of the time. However, you can make really good ones on special occasions, black Friday or holidays. So if you haven't bought yours, look for a deal this holiday season.

What Materials Are Cut by Cricut?

Hundreds of materials! You can cut a variety of materials with the Cricut machines and the following are some of them:

- Vinyl (permanent, Iron-on, removable, and glitter)
- Parchment paper
- Plain and corrugated paper
- Stick paper
- Cardstock (all kinds)
- Fabric
- Textile
- Faux leather
- Thin woods (by Cricut maker only)

And more!

Are Materials for Cricut Expensive?

Answer: Materials can be quite expensive, but it also depends on your projects. That's why it is important to buy that Cricut machine that will leave some money to buy materials and tools. Otherwise, it will be tough for you if you don't have an extra budget. Similarly, many wood materials are also expensive.

If you are a beginner, first focus on papercraft to learn everything about Cricut, make plenty of mistakes, and then move your way up.

Are Off-Brand Materials Compatible with Cricut?

Answer: Yes, they are. You don't have to limit yourself with the materials that the only Cricut makes. There are thousands of materials that are available online, on which you can experiment.

What is the Cricut Mystery Box?

Answer: Cricut releases the mystery box every month, which contains cool materials. You won't know what those materials are until you get that box. And the amazing part is that you will get more than what you have paid for. So, if you buy those materials, you have to pay a higher price, and then getting them together in the box.

The mystery box does run out, so make sure to get yours immediately at the beginning of the month.

What is the Cricut Adaptive Tool System?

Answer: It's a powerful feature of Cricut maker. It controls the direction of the blade and adjusts the pressure on it to match the blade with the material of your current project. This amazing tool system enables Cricut Maker to cut with ten times more force than any other machine in the Cricut Family. And that's why the Cricut Maker is able to cut materials like leather and wood easily.

Does It Print?

Answer: No, the Cricut machine is not a printer. Cricut does draw and create outlines like shapes, letters, etc.

Does It Need Ink?

Answer: Since Cricut doesn't print, it doesn't need ink. For drawing, you will require pens, and there are a variety of options from which you can choose yours.

Does It Laminate?

Answer: No, the Cricut machine doesn't laminate.

Does It Emboss?

Answer: Only Cricut Cuttlebug has the technology that enables it to emboss on the substrate. If you have any other Cricut from its family, then you can use stencils or workaround with other tools to emboss anything.

Does It Sew?

Answer: Cricut cuts fabric and textiles; it doesn't sew the fabrics.

Does It Cut Fabric?

Answer: You can work with a variety of fabrics and cut them in different sizes by using Cricut. For this, Cricut Maker is your best assistance. It allows you to cut textiles or fabric without any bonded materials. If you have Cricut from Cricut Explore machines, you have to bond it before cutting it. And, after cutting fabric from Cricut, you can proceed to sew it as your heart desires.

What is Backing Material?

Answer: Backing material is needed to cut fabric on the Cricut Explore family machines. Also known as heat and bond, it stabilizes the fabric on the mat and makes sure cutting is done automatically. If you don't adhere backing material to your fabric, the fabric won't cut properly and may ruin completely.

Does It Cut Wood?

Answer: It depends on the Cricut machine. Wood is only cut by Cricut Maker and that too only of some types like basswood and balsa. Cricut maker comes with a normal blade that is not enough to cut thick wood. You need to have a knife blade for cutting thick materials.

Troubleshooting Your Cricut Explore Air Machine

Problems with Printing Images

The Explore machine will work with a variety of printers, but some printers will jam when using card stock. The best option is to use a printer that feeds the card stock from the rear. The fewer turns the card stock makes in the printer, the less chance of it jamming.

Play it safe and don't use a laser printer for vinyl or sticky material. The heat of the printer will melt the material and could damage the printer.

Design Space has a printable area that is 6.75 by 9.25. This is a lot bigger than in past versions.

When you're working with an image you are going to print, select a square from the Shapes tool, and place it behind your image. Make the size of the square 6.75 and 9.25. Then you can clearly see while you're working with your image whether or not it is within the printable area. Make the square a light color so you can see it separate from your image.

You can put more than one image in the box. Attach the images so you can move them all at one time. Delete the box before printing.

It's easier than ever to create custom designs for multiple uses just by changing their Line type instead of redesigning the whole project.

Pens

When you're inserting a pen into your machine, place a piece of scrap paper under the pen. This keeps the pen from marking up your material or your machine when you click it into the clamp.

There are several ways to breathe new life into dried markers, sometimes just soaking the tip will work or refilling the pen with 90% alcohol.

Besides the homemade universal pen adapter I mentioned, the tube-shaped pencil grips fit some markers, making them compatible with the Explore.

Problems with Cutting Images

Before unloading the mat, try to determine if the material has been cut to satisfaction. If not, manually hit the cut button on the Explore and cut it again several times.

Use the Custom Material Settings in Design Space to increase or decrease the pressure, add multiple cuts, choose an intricate cut setting, or change materials. Within each category, there are several listings for different kinds of paper or card stock, for example. Just try selecting a different kind and see if that helps.

Tip: Create your own custom settings for any material by selecting Manage Custom Materials from the main menu. Then just click Add New Material and enter the information.

Some complex designs won't cut well in Fast Mode, so just cut it regularly. Make sure the blade and mat are clean.

If your images are not cutting correctly, be sure and wipe the mat and scrape off any access material left from previous projects. If the mat is severely scored or gouged, replace it.

Try switching to another mat, such as the stickier blue mat. If the mat isn't sticky enough, the material can slip and won't cut properly. Or tape the paper to the mat.

Then carefully clean the blade. If there is still a problem, it might be time to replace the blade. Using the new German Carbide blade is your best option for optimal cutting. Believe it or not, there can be a slight difference in the cutting edge between one new blade and another.

Make sure the blade fits tightly in the housing. Regularly clean out the blade housing of fibers that accumulate and interfere with the cutting process. Blow into the housing or use a straightened paperclip and carefully loosen any stuck material.

Since the angle of the deep cutting blade is different, try using it on regular material when experiencing problems.

If you get a message saying that the image is too large, you simply need to resize the image to make it smaller. Some people think that since the mat is 12 x 12, they can use 12 x 12 images. But there is a slight space left for margins, so the largest image size is 11.5 x 11.5. You can purchase a 12 x 24 mat to make larger cuts of 11.5 x 23.5.

If all else fails, try a different material. Some users find that certain brands of paper or card stock work better than others.

Mats

If your mat is too sticky when it's new, place a white T-shirt on it and press lightly or just pat it with your hands. This will reduce some of the stickiness.

When using a brayer and thin paper, don't apply a lot of pressure on the mat. This makes it hard to remove without ripping the paper.

Always clean your mat after each use. Use a scraper to remove small bits of lint or paper that have been left behind. These small scraps will cause problems with future projects.

You can wipe the mat with a damp cloth. Then replace the plastic cover between uses to prevent dust and dirt from sticking to the mat.

When the mat has lost its stickiness, tape the material to the mat around the edges or wash it with a little soap and water, rinse, let dry and it's good to go.

Have you seen those food-grade flexible cutting mats or boards? Some users are turning them into Cricut mats. Look for the thin plastic ones that are 12 x 12 or 12 x 24.

Use spray adhesive and cover the mat leaving a border, so the glue doesn't get on the rollers, or just spray the back of the card stock to adhere to the makeshift mat.

Load and Unload

When you load the mat into the Explore, always make sure that it's up against the roller wheels and under the guides. This assures the material will load straight when you press the load button.

When the cut is complete, never pull the mat out of the machine as this can damage the wheels. Always hit the unload button and then remove the mat.

To extend the life of the mat, turn it around, and load it from the bottom edge. Position the images on different parts of the mat instead of always cutting in the upper left corner.

Curling

Here's how to avoid curling material into a useless mess. When working with new mats, they tend to hold on for dear life.

When you're pulling a project off the mat, do not pull the paper (or whatever material) up and away from the mat. This will cause it to curl into a mess.

Instead, turn the mat over and curl it downward. Pull the mat away from the paper instead of pulling the paper up and away from the mat.

It seems like a slight difference, but it will save you from trying to uncurl and flatten a project. Just remember how curled the mat was when you first unboxed it, it had to wait till it flattened out.

Blades

When cutting adhesive material, glue accumulates on the blades and should be periodically removed. Dip a Q-Tip in nail polish remover to clean any sticky and build up residue. Check the cutting edge for nicks and that the tip is still intact.

Note: These blades are extremely sharp. Always use the utmost care when removing them or replacing them into your Cricut. Never leave them lying within reach of children. Save the tips and cap the blades before trashing them.

For best results use the German Carbide blades. The regular Cricut blades will fit in the Explore blade housing even though they're shaped differently.

At this time there is no German Carbide deep cut blade for the Explore. The blade that comes with the deep cut housing for the Explore is the regular deep cutting blade.

Materials

When you're planning a project with a new material it's good to do a small test first to make sure the material cuts the way you want. This will save you from potential problems and from wasting a large amount of material.

Try one of the in-between settings on the Smart Set Dial. Some card stock is thicker than other types, so you may need to adjust settings, use the multi-cut settings, or re-cut the image manually by hitting the cut button again.

By default, the Smart Set dial for paper, vinyl, iron-on, card stock, fabric, poster board has been set up to work best with Cricut products. Each material has three settings on the dial. If the cuts aren't deep enough, increase the pressure, or decrease the pressure if the cuts are too deep. For even more control, use the custom settings within Design Space.

Additionally, using a deep cutting blade (with the housing) or adjusting the stickiness of the mat may help.

Iron-on Vinyl

Sometimes the iron-on vinyl sticks to the iron. First, be sure your iron is not too hot. Follow the recommendations on the product. Make sure you purchased the type of vinyl that can be applied with an iron and not a professional heat press.

Next, try using parchment paper, a Teflon sheet, or a piece of cotton fabric between the vinyl and the iron. Use a firm heat resistant surface such as a ceramic tile or wooden cutting board to place your project on. Press and hold instead or ironing back and forth.

Always flip the image in Design Space. Put the shiny vinyl side down while cutting and the shiny side up when attaching to the material.

Iron-on Glitter Vinyl

When working with glitter vinyl I move the dial one notch passed iron-on vinyl toward light card stock. It seems to cut better using that setting.

After you make the first cut, do not remove the mat from the machine. Check to see if it cut through the vinyl. Sometimes I have to run it through one more time for a complete cut. Especially if it's a new brand I haven't worked with.

Stencils

There are many materials you can use to make stencils. Some users suggested plastic file folders that can be found cheaply at a Dollar Store. Another option is sending laminating sheets through a laminating machine and then putting them through your Cricut to cut the stencil. Run it through twice to make sure cuts are complete.

Problems with Machine Pausing

If your Cricut machine stops while cutting, writing, or scoring, I've already made several suggestions to correct the problem, here's another option.

Maybe the project itself, if it always happens, tries deleting that project and recreating it. Turn off your computer and disconnect from your machine. Turn off your Cricut machine and wait a few moments. Then restart and reconnect.

Problems with Bluetooth Wireless

If you're using an Explore Air or Explore Air 2 your Cricut machine is already Bluetooth enabled. But with an Explore or Explore One you will need to buy a Bluetooth adaptor.

When using Bluetooth be sure your machine is close, no more than 15 feet from the computer.

Make sure to verify your computer is Bluetooth enabled. If not, you'll need to buy a Bluetooth Dongle and place it in an unused USB port.

If you lose the Bluetooth connection, try uninstalling your Cricut under Bluetooth devices and then reinstalling.

Some people find their Design Space software works faster by using the USB cord instead of the Bluetooth connection.

CHAPTER 2:

Review of the Best Cricut Machine for Beginners: How to Use Them

Tips on How to Use the Cricut Explore Air Effectively

Want to enjoy your machine? Here are a few tips and tricks that will help you.

De-Tack Your Cutting Mat!

Your Cricut Explore Air will arrive with a cutting mat upon which you will put your projects before cutting. When purchased newly, the cutting mat is usually very sticky. I would advise that you prime the cutting mat before your first use. Priming makes it less sticky such that your paper projects do not get damaged. You prime the cutting mat by placing a clean, dry fabric over the cutting stock over the cutting mat and pulling it out again.

Keep Your Cutting Mat Clean

Use wipes to keep your cutting mat clean. Be careful with alcohol wipes as they could make the mat lose stickiness. You can also use the plastic cover to store your cutting mat when it is not in use.

Use the Proper Tools

Use the correct Cricut Tools. The best tools are the tools from the Cricut Tool Set. This toolset contains tweezers, scrapers, scissors, a spatula, and a weeding tool. These tools make work go very smoothly.

Start Your Cricut Journey with the Sample Project

It is best to start with the sample project and the material provided. The materials you will find in the package will be sufficient for you to start an initial sample project. Start with a simple sample project to have a feel of how the machine works.

Always Test Cuts

When carrying out projects, it is advisable to do a test cut before running the whole project. You can designate a simple cut to test run your settings before cutting material for the project. If the blade is not well set, the test cut will reveal it.

Replace Pen Lids After Use

Replace the pen lids when you are done using your pens. This avoids it from drying out. It is a good thing that Design Space sends a notification that reminds you to put the lid back on!

Link Your Old Cricut Cartridges

If you have cartridges you have used with your older machines, you can still hook them up with your new machine.

Bend the Cutting Mat to Get Materials off the Cutting Mat

To remove cut materials from the cutting mat (especially delicate Vinyl), you can bend the mat away from the material. That way, you can use the spatula to help get the cut material off the cutting mat.

Use the Deep Cut Blade for Thicker Materials

Use the deep cut blade to cut through thick materials. These materials could be leather, cardboard, or even chipboard. Get the blade and the blade housing.

Use Different Pens Where Necessary

Just like you use should use different blades for different materials, you should use different pens for different uses.

There are different pen adapters available which you can use with your machine.

Make Use of Free Fonts

There are many free fonts you can use. You can make use of these fonts for free instead of purchasing fonts on Cricut Access.

When you identify a desired free front, download it, and install it on your computer. The font will appear on Cricut Design Space.

Use Different Blades for Different Materials

Do not use one single blade for all the different materials you will cut. For example, you can have one blade for cardboard, another for only leather, and one for vinyl.

It is best to have different blades for different materials because each material wears differently on the blade. A dedicated blade will be best because it will be tuned to the peculiarities of each material.

Use Weeding Boxes for Intricate Patterns

When cutting delicate or intricate patterns it is important to use weeding boxes in the process.

Create a square or rectangle using the square tool in Cricut Design Space and place it such that all your design elements are all in it.

Doing this makes weeding easier as all your design elements are grouped within the square or rectangle you have created.

Always Remember to Set the Dial

This sounds like stating the obvious setting the dial to the right material is something you can easily forget. The consequences of forgetting to set the dial to the appropriate material range from damaged cutting mats to shallow cuts on the materials. You can prevent these by always setting the dial before cutting.

Other Tips & Tricks

Always clean your Cricut cutting mat after every project. Roll a lint roller over the Cricut mat to remove tiny leftovers of dirt and lint from the surface of the mat.

To make absolutely sure that you do not regret your action while using any Cricut machine, Cricut Explore Air 2 included, make it a habit of always testing the cutting of your material by using a small piece of the material you wish to cut first before cutting the main material. Watch out for these materials: wood, fabric, or felt because they present different challenges during the cut process.

When you want to detach your processed material from the cutting mat after unloading it, roll the Cricut mat backward away from the material instead of peeling the material away from the Cricut mat.

Always organize your blades and knives in a separate compartment or container. This will help you pick the correct blade or knife for a particular project because mixing them up may lead you to use an inappropriate blade for a project, which might result in blunting the blades or even outright damage.

Organize your Cricut tools so that they will not be flying everywhere around the project area to avoid messing up with your project or even causing you bodily harm. These tools include scissors, spatula, scoring tools, pic, weeding tools, etc.

You must keep your blades sharp every time so that you do not get your materials messed up while cutting and get them replaced when necessary.

Make sure that you dispose of the used ones properly to avoid injury to you and those around you, especially moms with little kids. I am sure you do not want your kids to get hurt from the blades.

Use this important resource from the makers of Cricut Explore Air 2; their website Cricut.com where you are granted access to many YouTube videos and project ideas. If you need more help, search for information on Google or Pinterest.

Using features such as fonts and a few projects on Cricut will cost you a few bucks, but you can cut this cost by subscribing to Cricut Access. With this, there is worry about cartridges, and all purchases will stay in your account.

If the cut edges of the material you are working on are rough and uneven, it simply means that the blade you are using is blunt. The solution is to replace the blade with another one.

If the material in the cutting mat moves while being cut, it means that your mat is not sticky enough. The solution is to replace your mat and the used material or use tape to hold your material firmly to the mat.

Best Tools and Software for Cricut Explore Air Machine

Cricut Design Space

The Cricut Mini was one of the first machines that worked with a computer. The design software it used was called Cricut Craft Room. Cricut Craft Room was the predecessor of Design Space. With the advancement in technology, the Cricut cutting machines also became more advanced. As the Cricut machines advanced, the design software needed to keep up with them. Cricut Craft Room was slowly phased out in 2018, and Design Space became the design software that is currently used with Cricut cutting machines.

With Design Space, there are unlimited possibilities. Depending on the cutting machine, some of the older design cartridges can still be used with the software.

Design Space has a library full of preloaded designs, templates, and images. You are not limited to using Design Space or Cricut images either. You can also upload your own images.

Getting Started with Cricut Design Space

Once you have downloaded Design Space, you will find it easy to learn the program. Design Space costs nothing to download and install. Although there are some designs, images, and fonts that are charged to your account, there are many free images, templates, shapes, and fonts.

Once you have a Design Space ID, you have access to the software's vast library of designs and all of its cutting capabilities. Design Space offers a limited-time free trial of Cricut Access, which is a membership-based library of images, designs, projects, and more.

The great thing about Design Space is that you do not have to have a Cricut Access membership to buy any of the projects, images, or designs. You can purchase them if and when you require them.

Cricut Design Space Quick Guide

This section will make more sense if you follow along with an open Design Space session.

Design Space Screens

There are two main screens for Design Space.

Home Screen

This is the first screen you will encounter when Design Space loads. You can click on any of the project windows in each section to access or view the projects.

The screen is split into the following sections:

- Top Menu Bar — This is the top, dark gray Menu bar. When you are on the Home screen, this menu bar will have the following options on it:
    - Home — This indicates the screen you are viewing.
    - Welcome <Name> message — This will have your login name.
    - My Projects — This will take you to the directory of your stored/saved projects.
    - Machine — This is the cutting machine selection menu. Once you have selected your default machine, the machine will be loaded every time you log in.
    - "New Project" button — This will send you to a clean Canvas screen to begin working on a new project.
- Top Drop-down Menu Bar (3 stripes in the top left-hand corner of the gray menu bar) — This menu has a list of common options that are discussed in the "Menu Bar" section of this chapter.
- My Projects — This will list all of your current projects.
- Cricut Access — This will list the latest ready-to-make projects from Cricut Access.

- My Ready-to-Make Projects — This section selects ready-to-make projects for you, based on your latest projects.
- Other promotional sections — There are a few sections that display the latest projects and materials available to you.

Canvas Screen

This is the Design Screen where you will create all of your projects.

The Canvas screen is split into the following sections:

- Top Menu Bar — This is the top, dark gray Menu bar. When you are on the Canvas screen, this menu bar will have the following options on it:
    - Canvas — This indicates the screen you are viewing.
    - Untitled — This will remain "Untitled" until you have saved your current project. If you load a saved project, it will list the name of the opened project.
    - My Projects — This will take you to the directory of your stored/saved projects.
    - Save — This is the save button for your project. Once a project has been saved, there will be a second option listed "Save As." The "Save As" option is there, so you can save a project as another name and keep the current one intact.
    - Machine — This is the cutting machine selection menu. Once you have selected your default machine, it will load every time you log in.
    - "Make it" button — This button sends your current project to the "Prepare" screen to ready your design for cutting.

- Top Drop-down Menu Bar (3 stripes in the top left-hand corner of the gray menu bar) — This menu has a list of common options that are discussed in the "Menu Bar" section of this chapter.

- The Design Panel — This is the selection panel on the left-hand side of the screen. The Design Panel is where you can select the object you are going to use for your design projects. These objects include Templates, Projects, Images, Text, Shapes, and an option to upload your own designs.

- Edit Menu — This menu can be found below the top gray menu bar. It should be noted that this menu bar can change slightly depending on the object being designed. Some of the common features of this menu are:

  - Undo/Redo option — The first items on the left of the Edit menu are the Undo and Redo arrows. They are grayed out until there is an object on the screen or until an object has been changed. This is handy when you accidentally move, delete, or resize something on the screen.

  - Linetype — This is where the image or design linetype is determined. The default is always set to "Cut." The "Draw" option is for use with the Cricut Ink Pen accessories. The "Score Line" option is for marking a fold in the material.

  - The Linetype Color Swatch block — This is the small square next to the Linetype options. This option is used to determine what the color of the line will be.

  - Fill — The Fill option is used to change the color of the object on the screen. It is also where you will set the object to "Print." These are for features called "Print" and "Cut." This is when you send an image to the inkjet printer before cutting the material. It is for when you have various shapes, images, or objects that need to be drawn before they are cut.

- The Fill Color Swatch block — This changes the fill color of the chosen object on the screen.
- Select — This option will "Select All" images on the screen. Once the images have been selected, this option changes to "Deselect."
- Edit — This is the standard editing menu that contains the "Cut," "Copy," and "Paste" options.
- Align — This option aligns selected images either horizontally or vertically or centers them. It also contains a "Distribute" option, which equally spaces out images either vertically or horizontally.
- Arrange — This arranges the order of the objects.
- Flip — This "Flips" the object either vertically or horizontally. It also rotates it by 90°.
- Size — This option resizes the selected image(s).
- Rotate — This option allows you to rotate objects to a certain angle. It allows for some interesting object positioning on the screen.
- Position — This will place a selected object at the desired coordinates.

- The Layers and Color Sync panel — This is the panel found on the right-hand side of the Canvas screen. It is broken into two tabs.
    - Layers tab — The layers tab has a menu with the following options at the top:
        - Group — Objects that need to be kept together on the screen to be moved, marked, colored, etc., are easier to work with when they are grouped.
        - Ungroup — Ungroup is grayed out until objects have been grouped. Ungroup disconnects Grouped objects.
        - Duplicate — This option is used to clone selected objects and make an exact replica of them.
        - Delete — This option is used to delete selected objects.
    - Color Sync tab — This tab is useful when you have objects that you want to be drawn or printed in the exact same color. It will list the exact colors of all the objects on the screen for you to match other objects with.
    - Canvas Objects — The panel beneath the Layers panel menu lists all the objects currently on the design screen. As you get more familiar with working in Design Space, you will find this panel very useful.
    - Bottom Menu of the Layers/Color Sync panel — The bottom section of this panel has the following options:
        - Canvas — This hides or unhides any embedded objects on the Canvas, such as templates or background color.
        - Slice — This is for slicing up an object on the canvas.

        - Weld — Welds two objects together to form an outline.
        - Attach — Attaches objects on the screen that need to be printed together.
    - Flatten — Flattens an image with multiple parts into a single image.

- The Design Canvas — This is the graphed space in the middle of the screen where you will do all of your designs. It is set in inches as a default, but the settings can be customized through the top right-hand Dropdown menu discussed in the next section.
    - The Zoom Control is at the right-hand corner bottom of the Canvas. This is grayed out until you hover the mouse cursor over it. By default, it is set to 100% scale. You can set it to zoom in or out of the screen by using the + and - selection icons on each side of the current zoom % marker.

Prepare Screen

This is a screen that you will get to when you are ready to start cutting the project and have pressed the "Make it" button.

- Top Gray Menu — The Dropdown menu on the left of this menu only has one option when you are at the "Prepare" screen, that is to take you back to the Canvas. The name of the menu changes to "Prepare," and next to the name you will see the number of machine mat changes the project requires (1 mat). There will be the name of the project and the name of the cutting machine.

- The left-hand panel has the following options:
    - Project copies — This must not be confused with the number of cuts. This option will duplicate the design objects according to the amount selected.
    - Small Mat image — Depending on the number of machine mats required for the project, you could see a number of these small mats. This is where you select the mat you want to edit, rearrange, etc. Next to the mat, it will tell you if the machine is going to cut or draw the object. It may also indicate if the object is to be printed.
    - Material Size — Here you can select the material size. This helps to cut down on using unnecessary material.
    - Mirror — The sliding button next to this option will turn mirroring on or off. Mirroring turns the objects on the mats upside down.
    - Machine Mats — In the middle of the screen, you will find an exact replica of the machine mat and how the design is placed to be cut. You can move objects around the screen to position them for cutting.
    - Cancel button — In the bottom right-hand corner of the screen, you will find the "Cancel" button. This button will cancel the cut and return you to the Design Canvas screen.
    - Continue button — In the bottom right-hand corner of the screen is the "Continue" button. This takes the cutting to the next stage. You will be prompted to load the accessories in the cutting machine, select the material being used, and load the machine mat.

Menu Bars

There are two main menu bars that the Home screen, Canvas, and Prepare screens have in common. These menus are:

Top Menu Bar

This is the dark gray menu bar that changes slightly depending on the screen you are in. This menu bar has been discussed alongside the relevant screens.

Top DropDown Menu Bar

Next to the screen name on the gray menu bar, there are three horizontal lines. These lines represent a dropdown menu. This menu is the same for the Home screen and the Canvas screen. The Prepare screen is slightly different (see the Prepare screen for details). The Drop-down menu options are as follows.

- View Profile
    - You can upload a profile picture.
    - You have 350 characters to write something about yourself.
    - This is where you can access your saved projects.
- Home
    - When you select this option, it will return you to the Home screen.
- Canvas
    - When you select this option, it will return you to the Canvas screen.

- New Machine Setup
    - This option lists all the compatible machine types to choose from.
    - You can install the chosen cutting machine.
    - The EasyPress 2 option is for the updating of the EasyPress2 firmware and requires a USB cable.
- Calibration
    - This option is to calibrate the cutting machine blades.
    - This option also calibrates the printer attached to the cutting machine.
- Manage Custom Materials
    - This is where you can find a list of custom materials based on the type of cutting machine you have connected to Design Space.
- Update Firmware
    - You should check for firmware updates for your cutting machine on a regular basis.
- Account Details
    - This is the section where you can manage your Cricut account details.
- Link Cartridges
    - This is where you can link design cartridges, should the cutting machine support them.

- Cricut Access
  - This is where you set up and manage your Cricut Access account.
- Settings
  - Language — This is where you can set the software to your desired language. The default language selection is English.
  - Canvas grid — This is where you can customize how you would like the Design Canvas grid to look. You can use the Full Grid, Partial Grid, or No Grid.
  - Units — This option allows you to set the units of measure for Design Space from Imperial to Metric.
  - Saving for Offline — This is where you can set your projects to save only to the cloud or allow for offline saving to your hard drive.
- Legal
  - Cricut Legal page: This includes the Cricut Terms of Use, Terms, and Conditions, Privacy Policy, Patents, Online Policies, Cricut Access Policy, and so on.
- New Features
  - This option gets updated with new updates and versions of the Design Space software. It informs you of what changes were made and what changes are to come.

- Country
    - This is automatically detected, but you can set it manually as well. This is the country where you are currently located.
- Help
    - There is a lot of helpful documentation and various articles online to assist you with various aspects of Design Space.
- Sign Out
    - This is where you can sign out of your current Design Space session.
- Feedback
    - You can have your say on any of the new features or regarding how you like Cricut Design Space using this option.

When you read through all these Design Space menus, features, and options, it can seem quite daunting. Don't worry. When you start working with the machine and doing some of the beginner projects, the screens will start to make a bit more sense to you.

Cricut Explore Air Project Ideas

Selecting Pens to Be Used with the Cricut Machine

The pens used in the Cricut Explore machines are specially made for them and are not compatible with any other mechanisms that you might decide to use them with.

Loading and unloading the pen into the Cricut Explore Air machine

Note that the Cricut Explore One machine will require you to purchase a separate accessory adapter to have a chance to use the Cricut pens.

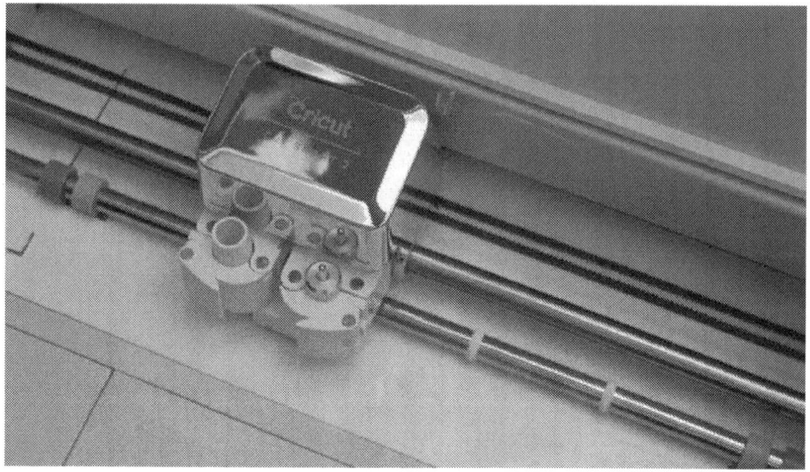

Before you start the writing process with the Cricut Explore Air machine, you will need to have your image or text set to "Write" instead of having it in the cut mode. The "Line Type of the image and text" might need to be altered to get this done.

To load or unload your pen into the Cricut Explore Air 2 machine, you are required to take the following steps:

- Go to accessory clamp A and get it opened.
- Get the cap detached from the pen.
- Hold the accessory clamp in the upward direction while inserting the pen down in the housing until you can no longer see the arrow on the pen.
- Close the clamp once the pen has been inserted.

- As soon as you are done with the writing process, you can now open the accessory clamp and have the pen pulled upward to get it removed.

- Fix back the cap to the pen to prevent it from drying out.

Pairing the Cricut Machine Through Bluetooth to the Computer

To get your Cricut Explore Air 2 paired with your computer or mobile device, you are required to take the following steps:

- Make sure your Wireless Bluetooth Adapter is in place and working.

- Have the Cricut Explore Air 2 turned on, and it should be at most 15 feet from your PC.

- Check to be sure your computer is Bluetooth enabled by taking the following sub-steps on your computer.

    - Go to the "Start button" and right-click on it.

    - Select the "Device Manager."

    - If you have the Bluetooth listed in the device manager, Bluetooth is definitely enabled; otherwise, you will have to get a USB device referred to as Bluetooth Dongle to get your computer interacting with other Bluetooth devices.

- You can now close your Device manager once you have confirmed it is Bluetooth enabled.

- Go to the "Start menu."

- Select "Settings."

- Go to the "Devices" option and open it.
- Make sure the Bluetooth is active and select "Include Bluetooth or another device.
- Click on "Bluetooth," you can then grab a cup of coffee while your PC searches for and pairs with the Cricut Machine.
- Select the Cricut machine once it appears on the list.
- In a case where you are prompted to input in a PIN, type in 0000 and click on "Connect."
- Once you select the Connect option, your Cricut Explore Air 2 machine will now be paired to your computer.

Note:

The Cricut Explore Air 2 machine might show up as an Audio on the Bluetooth list. If this happens, it's okay, and you can go ahead with pairing.

In a situation where you have multiple Cricut machines, make use of the device code in identifying which one you like to pair. The device code can be found on the serial number tag at the bottom of the machine.

Unpairing or Removing the Bluetooth Device

The removal or unpairing of your Bluetooth device from the Cricut Explore Air 2 varies based on the version of the operating system in use. You are required to take the following steps in the process of unpairing or removing the Bluetooth device:

- Go to the Start menu
- Select Settings

- Select the Devices option
- Choose the device you want to remove and click on the "Remove device."
- You will be prompted to confirm your action.

Resetting the Cricut Explore Air 2 Machine

When some issues arise with your machine, there might be a need to perform a hard reset for such a problem to be solved. In performing the hard reset, you are required to take the following steps:

- Turn off the Cricut Explore Air 2 machine.
- Simultaneously hold down the Magnifying glass, pause as well as the power buttons.
- Hold the three buttons down simultaneously until the machine displays a rainbow screen, and you can release the buttons afterward.
- Promptly follow the on-screen instructions that follow.
- Get the process repeated one more time.

Finding the Current Firmware Version on My Machine

It is recommended to have the updated version of the firmware of your device for optimal effective use. This part of the book helps with the latest firmware version that is available for all the Cricut machines.

- Make sure you have your Cricut Explore machine connected and powered on.
- Sign in to the Cricut Design Space.

- Go to the upper left corner of the Design space and select the account menu.
- Select the "Update Firmware"
- You will be prompted with a pop-window, select your machine out of the dropdown list and give the software a few moments to detect your machine.
- You will receive a message letting you know if your firmware is up to date or not once your machine has been detected. If your machine is not up to date, you will be notified of any available updates.

Here is the list of the latest firmware versions:

- Cricut Explore: 1.091
- Cricut Explore Air: 3.091
- Cricut Explore Air 2: 5.120
- Cricut Explore one: 2.095
- Cricut Maker: 4.175

It is to be noted that the Cricut Explore Air or Cricut Maker firmware can also be checked using the Design Space on the computer.

The Fast Mode of the Cricut Explore Air Machine and How It Is Used

The Cricut Explore Air 2 machine is designed to work in the fast mode, which allows the machine to cut and write up to two times faster than we have in the previous Cricut Explore models.

The fast mode is also employed in the Cricut Makers machines as well.

The Fast mode features are made available with the Iron-on, Vinyl, and Cardstock material settings, which are set to Vinyl to Cardstock+ on the Smart Set dial available on the Explore machine.

To make use of the Fast Mode feature of the Cricut Explore Air machine, here are the basic instructions that you will need to follow:

- When all is set for writing and cutting your project, simply go to the Cut screen.

- The Fast Mode option will be made available if you have chosen the right material for the mode.

- Toggle the switch to the "ON" position by clicking or tapping the switch to get the Fast Mode activated. It is to be noted that the Cricut Explore Air 2 machines tend to make a louder noise while making use of the fast mode features; this is normal.

Choosing the Material Settings

As earlier said, it is advisable always to get a test cut done using a small piece of your material before cutting out your project to make sure your cut settings have been appropriately chosen on your material.

The Smart Set dial is used for the selection of material, which helps in offering pre-defined settings to enable you to get the best results using your paper, cardstock, iron-on, fabric, etc.

The Smart Set dial compensates for having to employ pressure, speed adjustments, depth manually because all you will have to do here is to switch the dial to the material type in use and apply the GO button.

Custom Cut Settings of the Cricut Machine

The Cricut Explore Air 2 machine is made up of seven preset dial options, which are the light cardstock, paper, Vinyl, Iron-on, Bonded fabric Cardstock, and posterboard. Situations do arise where the materials you are working on are not available on the dial; in such cases, take the following steps:

- Go to Design Space.
- Select the project.
- Select "Make it."

A drop-down menu will show up where you will be able to select your material.

The Smart Set dial is made up of seven pre-loaded material settings, including a Custom option. The half-step settings which are located between the material markings are used for increasing and decreasing pressures.

We have the half-step settings located in between the Fabric and Custom, and it is used to direct the machine to cut twice in the same spot.

Using or Creating Custom Material Settings

The Cricut Explore Air machines are used for cutting different kinds of materials. It is designed with pre-programmed settings on the design space to create flexibility when working on projects using various materials. Apart from these pre-programmed settings, you can create your own as well.

Making use of Custom material settings

- Get signed in to the Design Space and create a project.
- Turn on your Cricut Explore machine.
- Have your Cricut Explore machine connected to your computer.
- Go to the Project Preview screen and ensure that the Smart Set Dial is appropriately locked to Custom.
- Click on "Browse All Materials."

You can simply search for the material by name or scrolling to browse the list. Note that all the materials having the Cricut logo next to them are the Cricut branded materials.

How to Create a New Custom Material

This becomes handy in a situation where your choice of material is not available on the materials list. When this happens, you can simply try the settings that have the closest match to your material or build a new setting.

It is important to note that new Custom materials cannot be added in the Cricut Design space when making use of the Android device, but any materials that are added from the Computer, iPhone, or iPad will be made available on the Android app.

To create a new material setting, you are required to take the following steps below:

- Go to the menu and select the "Manage Custom Materials" or select the "Materials Settings" located at the bottom of the page when browsing materials for projects to gain access to the Custom Materials screen.

- Select the "Add New Material" by scrolling down to the bottom of the list.

- Have the name of the material indicated.

- Click on the "Save" option.

- After saving the material, you will have the chance to make necessary adjustments with the use of the following:

    - Multi-cut: This helps in directing the machine to cut multiple times in the same image, and it is usually used for thick materials.

    - Cut pressure: This adjusts the slider or using the +/- buttons.

    - Blade type: You can select from the deep-point blade or high-grade Fine-Point blade for the Design Space to prompt accordingly.

    - Select "Save" to get your new custom material saved after configuration.

    - Close the materials screen with the “X” sign that will be found at the top-right corner.

After this, your new material will be found in the materials list and can be found making use of the search option. It is to be noted that the star can be used in adding the material to your favorite.

Getting Custom Materials Edited and Deleted

To edit or delete your custom material, you are required to take the following steps:

- Open the Menu.
- Click on the "Manage Custom Materials."
- Scroll down to the material
- Select the Edit button.
- Edit or delete.

Important instructions to note during the creation of the custom settings

The thicker or denser materials may require a multi-cut to ensure that a complete cut-through is achieved but may not always need more pressure.

Anytime a new custom material setting is being created, it is advisable to always refer to the material settings that closely match your choice to have an inkling of the amount of pressure and the varying cut setting that will be needed for an effective result. It is important to note that the maximum thickness of a custom material should be less than 2.0mm for the Cricut Explore machine and the Cricut Maker machine; it is less than 2.4mm.

You are advised to have several tests carried out to help in adjusting pressure or multi-cut settings for the desired results to be achieved.

The Removal and Replacement of the Accessory Adapter for the Cricut Explore Air 2 Machine

It is important to note that the accessory adapters of Cricut machines are different from each other. For the Explore One, we have the accessory adapter switched with the blade housing for the writing or scoring process, while for the Explore Air 2 and some other Cricut machines, we have the accessory adapter housed in its clamp, which is separate from the blade housing.

The accessory Clamp A of the Cricut Explore Air 2 machine has the accessory adapter pre-installed in them. To insert a pen, you don't have to remove the accessory adapter; nevertheless, if you want to remove the accessory adapter for other purposes, you are required to take the following steps:

- Get the accessory Clamp A opened.
- Have your thumb placed underneath the adapter and apply pressure in the upward direction while you push down on the clamp. This will result in the accessory clamp pooping out.

Have a finger placed underneath accessory clamp A to stabilize while reinserting the accessory adapter from the top to have the accessory adapter reinstalled.

You will need to get some pressure applied in the process of inserting the adapter. The adapter should automatically snap into place if the installation is done correctly.

Installing the Bluetooth Adapter of the Cricut Explore Machine

It is to be noted that the Cricut Maker, Explore Air, as well as the Explore Air 2 machine, are made up of an inbuilt Bluetooth; therefore, they will not require a Bluetooth adapter.

To install the Bluetooth adapter in the Explore or Explore One machine, you are required to take the following steps:

- Turn the Explore or Explore One machine on.
- Detach the cap from the Bluetooth adapter.
- Have the adapter inserted into the Explore while the text Cricut faces up. The adapter takes about 2/3rd of the way into the machine once it is inserted.
- As soon as the blue light of the adapter shows up, it can't be pushed in any further. The blue light is an indicator that it has been correctly installed.

Check To Ensure Your Cricut Toolset Is Complete

A complete Cricut Toolset should contain a scraper, tweezers, weeding tool, a spatula, and scissors, so you should make sure you have these tools available.

The Cricut Scoring Stylus

The Cricut Scoring Stylus is an essential tool, especially for your card projects. So at the time of purchase, it is necessary to check to make sure this tool comes with the Cricut machine.

How to Make a Customized Graphic T-Shirt

Among the projects you can do with your Cricut machine, I am super excited about this one; T-shirt. Maybe because I wear it always or because of the different creative expressions on it or the fact that it is a money-spinning business concept. I hope that by the time you go through this step-by-step approach, you will be as excited as I am. Let me begin the step-by-step approach:

1. Open a new project on your Canvas
2. Click on Templates to picture your projects. Under Templates are different T-shirt designs, including Classic T-shirt, V-neck T-shirt, wide neck T-shirt, etc. Click on anyone you prefer.

You can alter the color using the toolbar in the top corner of your screen. This will help you to picture your design properly. So, if you are using a black T-shirt, change the color to black.

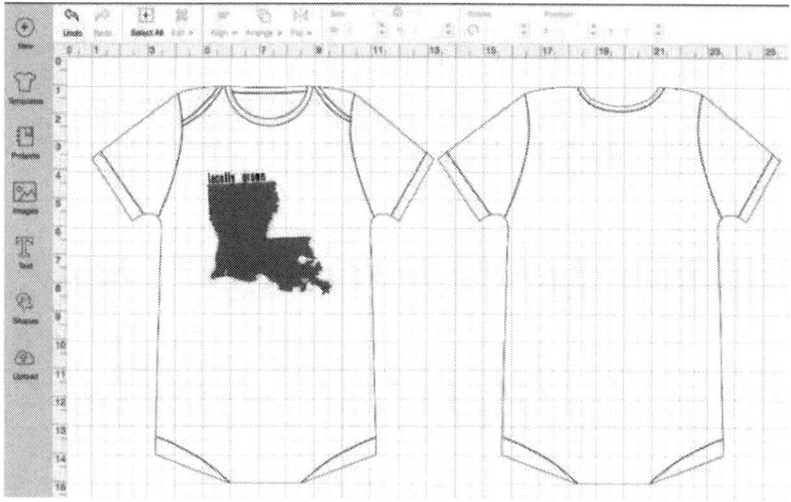

1. To get an image of the T-shirt, click on Images. Type in the text that defines your image in the top right corner of the search box. For instance, unicorns. Use a filter to thin down your search, click on Printables, then click on your preferred Unicorn image, and insert it to your Canvas.
2. If you can't find any image that suits you, there is another substitute; Google. Navigate to Google and search for unicorns, select images, and there are lots of them to choose from. Right click on it and save it to your device. The only problem with this method is that it is only for personal use. If you wish to sell it,

then you will require a commercial license for that. To use your downloaded image in your Canvas is super simple:

a. Click Upload
b. Click Upload Image.
c. Search for the downloaded image and open it.
d. Click on Complex.
e. Click Continue.
f. Clean the unicorn image.
g. Click preview button to picture your final cut image.
h. Click Continue.
i. Select Print and Cut images and then click Save.
j. Select the image you just uploaded in the library, then click Insert images.

3. If you wish, you can print your customized image without using designed images in the library or online download. How you do that is very simple:

a. Click Shapes.
b. Choose any image of your choice. For instance, the heart.
c. Take the image over the T-shirt and resize it to 6.5" or less.
d. Go to Fill menu and select Print.

e. Fill your shapes with different patterns on the Design Space by clicking on the Grey button at the top left side of the window, select pattern from the dropdown menu to show super amazing patterns.

f. Use any of the images that satisfy your design goal and edit it.

g. You can customize your image using text. Select Text, type in the letters, word, or sentence, then select your desired fonts.

h. Move the text, word, or sentence over your image and resize it.

i. Your Print Then Cut images will be shown on the Layer's panel.

4. Resize the image to fit in your T-shirt. Traditionally, your Print Then Cut image size should be equal or smaller than 6.7" x 9.2".

5. Drag it to the middle of your T-shirt.

6. If your unicorn image has more than one layer, then you need to flatten it. To do that select all the layers in the Layer's panel and click Flatten in the bottom right corner of your screen.

7. Delete all layers except the default flattened layer.

8. Go to the LineType menu on top of the window to make sure that the first box is set to Cut, and the fill box is set to Print.

9. Click Make It to display the mat preview area with a black box border.

10. Click Continue to move to the Print and Cut page.

11. You can use any of these fabrics: transfer medium for light-colored fabrics or medium for dark-colored fabrics.

    a. For light-colored fabrics, you need to mirror your image. Open a new window by clicking the Edit link in the top left corner of the window. On the new window, make sure that your image is toggled, and then Click Done.

    b. For dark-colored medium, you do not need to mirror your image. So, set it to Off.

12. Click Send to Printer and make sure that the Add Bleed option is enabled. Click the advance option and ensure that the quality is set to high quality, transfer medium type set to the appropriate one, and finally click on Print to send it to your printer.

13. The inkjet printer is recommended for this project. Do not use the laser printer because it is not compatible with this project. Select the correct transfer medium for the printer and load it into the printer. Put your transfer medium properly so that you do not print on the wrong side.

14. Now, go back to the Design Space, click on Browse All Materials, look for printable iron-on, choose your desired transfer medium, and then click Done.

15. Put the transfer medium in the left corner of your mat, load it into your Cricut machine, and then cut your decal.

16. Carefully weed your printed transfer medium beginning from the external transfer medium around your decal. Do not remove the decal from the back if you wish to use the light-colored transfer medium. For dark-colored transfer medium, you only remove your decal from the back.

17. Now, it is time to iron-on the decal unto your T-shirt. There are two methods to do the iron-on subject to the transfer medium.

a. For light-colored transfer medium: press the front of your T-shirt first, then place the decal on the T-shirt with the backing facing you. Make sure that the decal is placed in the middle of your T-shirt. Use your EasyPress to press the decal on your T-shirt gently, for about two minutes, at 300°C. Remove the backing immediately after finishing your ironing using the EasyPress

b. For dark-colored transfer medium: The first thing to do is press your T-shirt, then place your decal on it with the decal facing you. Cover the decal with a tissue paper, set the EasyPress to 300°C, then place the EasyPress over the tissue paper for about 30 seconds. Remove the iron and the tissue paper to reveal your decal on your T-shirt. If the edges are not properly attached to your T-shirt, repeat the ironing again for another 30 seconds.

How to Make Stickers with Cricut

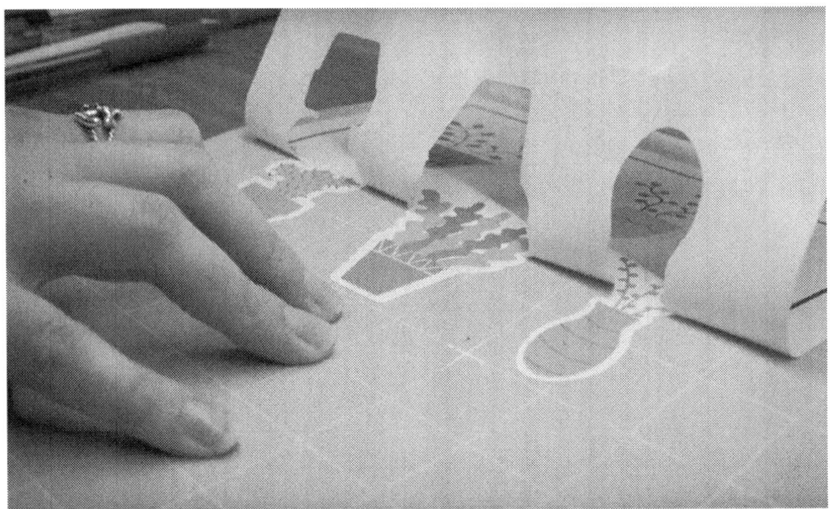

The first thing is to design your write up in your Design Space. The next thing is to follow these steps below to achieve your aim of getting amazing expressions at your desired object, in this case, a mug.

Measure the width of your mug so that you know the appropriate size to use in your Cricut Design Space.

Send it to your mat. The appropriate mat for this project is the Standard Grip mat

Click Continue

Select the material to be used. Go to the All Materials button and click on it if you don't have it listed on the screen. Your machine should be blinking by now.

Cut the appropriate size of vinyl material to be placed on the mat. The appropriate size is based on the size of your write-up as obtained in your Cricut Design space

Click on the Load button and then press the flashing Cricut button to load and cut your image for you. Note that your Cricut machine will notify you, through your Design Space app, if you are not using the right blade. You may be asked to identify the blade you intend to use.

When done, press the Unload button and remove your mat from the Cricut machine.

Remove your vinyl from the mat and use your weeding tools to remove the tiny pieces between your letters. Make sure you don't leave any unwanted piece to your letters because it might make all your effort to be unsatisfactory. Therefore, take your time to remove them.

When you have finished removing the little pieces from your letters, use the transport tape to pick up your design from the paper. Cut the appropriate size of transport tape in order not to waste it. Also, ensure that you peel off your transport tape before picking up your design. One good thing about the transport tape is that you can reuse it for other projects until it loses its adhesive power.

Pull the transport tape to pick up your design.

Place on your desired object, including mugs, wine glasses, etc. Use your scraper to remove any air bubble or stretch the edges of your object.

Finally, pull the transport tape from its edge from your object to leave your amazing write-ups to your object.

This is super exciting. I love to add little things that change the appearance of my mugs, utensils, wine glasses, jugs. The eye appeal is so amazing. And coupled with the fact that I can change the write-up and shapes on objects, especially during festive periods (such as Christmas, New Year, anniversaries, birthday celebration), makes me look forward to such experiences. I know you will love it too.

How to Make DIY Paper Succulent with Your Cricut

Flowers are beautiful, and they make our environment look amazing. Whether live or artificial, they serve the same purpose. Paper flowers and paper succulents provide a means of artificial flower for our environment, especially interior décor. You will definitely fall in love with this amazing project for both kids and beginners.

The materials for this super exciting project include the Cricut Explore machine, cardstock, foam mountain tape, different shades of green paint, and a paintbrush.

1. Design the cardstock using Cricut Design Space. Of course, you know how to customize or choose from the list of designs in your library.

2. Remove the succulent shapes from the cardstock

3. Use a dry brush and color paint to beautify your succulent leaves. Make use of a slight stroke of light shade and medium shade color at the tip and edge of the succulent leaves respectively.

4. Curve the succulent leaves gently with your fingers, turning the leaves upward.

5. Use foam mounting tape to join each of the succulent layers together. Ensure there is a separation between layers to make it realistic when you view it.

6. Place it on top of a craft cup wrapped with a colored cardboard sheet to give it an amazing view. I know you will love this project when you start to play with the number of options available for this craft.

How to Make Fabric Bookmark Using Your Cricut Machine

This project is super simple and will be a good way to start learning crafts for beginners and kids, I am particularly interested in this bookmark project because of the different colors and designs available for this project as well as its application. Without much story, let me walk you through how you are going to make your fabric bookmark. You will definitely fall in love with it as I have.

1. Cut your fabric to your desired size, keeping in mind the size of your mat. I suggest 2.5" x 7.5" fabric for every bookmark. Fit as many as you can on your FabricGrip cutting mat.

2. Use your Design Space to create a fusible cardboard using the size 6.70" high x 1.7" wide each. This should be done for each bookmark.

3. Load the fusible cardboard into your Cricut Explore machine and cut it. The fusible cardboard should be thick to give your bookmark strength.

4. Attach the wrong sides of your fabric together using clips or pins, then sew them at the longer side and the bottom.

5. Turn out your fabric bookmark casing using a pen or pencil to straighten the edges. Use pressing iron or EasyPress to press the bookmark you straightened out.

6. Insert the fusible cardboard into the bookmark casing.

7. Fold the open part of your bookmark casing and then press it with EasyPress or pressing iron.

8. Sew the part that has not been sewed back, stitching both ends.

9. Finally, press the whole bookmark with your EasyPress or pressing iron to make it tidy.

I have tried to make it simple and straightforward so that you can bring your own design and materials to reality for friends and loved ones and even personal bookmarks. There are many bookmark templates from the Cricut Library that you can play with.

How to Make a Frosty Wreath

Frosty wreaths are beautiful crafts for wall decals and door decorations for festivals like Christmas. You can use them for gifts, sell them, and even make them for home décor.

Materials for this project include Cricut Explore machine, FabricGrip, and StrongGrip mats, Cricut Felt, Knife Blade, Rotary Blade + accessories, vine wreath, glue, masking tape, chipboard, and Fabric Brayer.

Allow the chipboard to acclimatize to its environment for about 24 hours to avoid bending or warping.

Smooth the chipboard on the StrongGrip mat using a Brayer to adhere properly.

Use masking tape to secure the edges of the chipboard to the StrongGrip mat

Push the star wheels on the machine to the side, so they don't run on the chipboard, leaving traces behind.

The Knife Blade can only cut designs less than 10.5" and larger than 0.75". Anything more than that will destroy your blade.

Pause the Cricut Explore machine frequently to check the progress by lifting the edge of the chipboard.

To save your StrongGrip mat from wear, use a knife tool to cut the remaining when the Cricut machine has almost cut through your design.

Now time for the project. I expect that you know how to design the text for the chipboard in the Design Space so, I will not go there again.

This is helpful to avoid stuck pieces that can damage the Rotary Blade. When it is almost cut through, unload the mat and use the knife tool to cut the remaining chipboard to save your mat from wear.

Load the second chipboard piece for the snowflakes and follow step 2 to remove the stuck piece and knife blade to finish the segments of the snowflakes not cut through.

Use any color of your choice to paint the snowflakes, depending on how you want the final appearance of the project to look like.

For the felt snowflakes, set the material to Felt and use the same method for the chipboard to prepare the felt on the mat, this time FabricGrip mat. Please be careful with the dimension of the felt snowflakes so that you don't experience challenges cutting and removing them from the FabricGrip mat. Also, scrape them gently from the mat as the cut material can break easily.

Use the glue to attach them together on the 8" vine wreath to taste and enjoy your beautifully designed and crafted frosty wreath.

Faux Leather Bracelet Cricut Tutorial: How to Make It

The Cricut Explore Air 2 can be pretty amazing in doing a variety of things. One of those things is being able to make a leather bracelet with your Cricut. You can make pretty cool designs that you can turn into wearable pieces of jewelry.

To make a leather bracelet, you need your Cricut Explore Air 2, a deep point blade, faux leather, marker, ruler, craft knife, bracelet cut file, transfer tape, and a grip mat. You will also need glue, an EasyPress or iron, and an SVG design to crown it up.

Follow these steps to create your leather bracelets.

1. Log into your Design Space account menu.
2. Select "Canvas."
3. Upload an art set from Jen Goode into the Design Space. The Jen Goode is a set of designs with 4 different image layouts.
4. Ungroup the designs and hide the layers you don't require after selecting your design.
5. Create a base cut of the shape you want to use. Use a cut file and create the shape you want. For example, you can use a shape tool to create a circular design.
6. Add circle cutouts with basic shapes. Duplicate the layer so that you will use it for the back of the bracelet.
7. Set your iron or EasyPress ready and apply the vinyl to the uppermost layer of your leather.
8. Spread a thin coat of glue on the back of the duplicated layer and press it with the other layer together.
9. Add your bracelet strap or chain together with some other ornaments.
10. Congratulations! You have just made your first leather bracelet.

Note: You can make your layer as thick as you want it. Just apply the glue appropriately to put them together.

How to Make Planner Stickers with Cricut

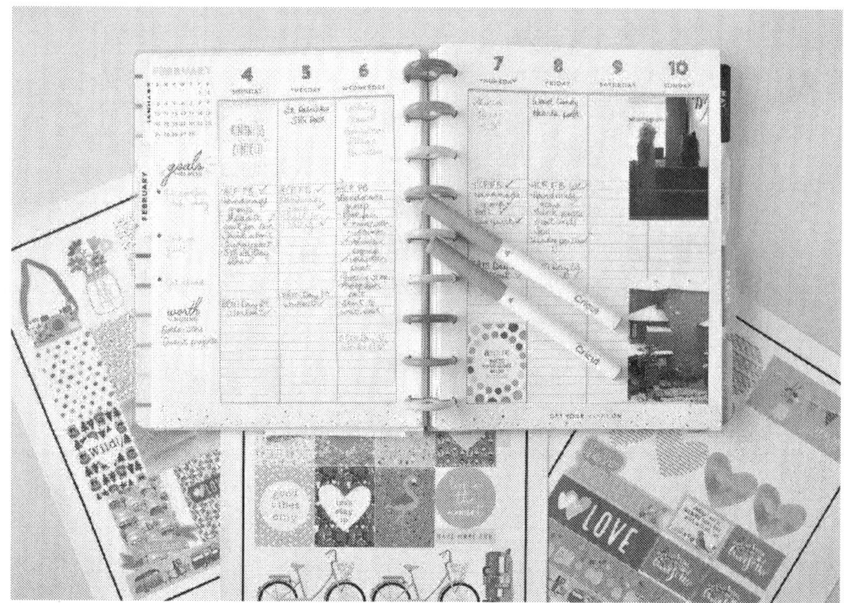

Planner stickers are more like reminders for events as they help to organize your activities. The materials for this project include: Cricut Explore Air machine, StandardGrip cutting mat, printable sticker paper,

Navigate to your Cricut Design Space and open it.

Select a shape, for instance, square or rectangle. Alternatively, select a square, then use the unlock dimension button to unlock its parameters, and finally resize it using the arrows to your desired values.

Use the design features discussed above to design your shape to fill, choose and edit pattern, add overlay(s) where you will input your text, select your desired fonts to use in typing your text to your sticker. Continue the editing until you get your desired design.

Note that you can still edit your sticker at this stage by clicking on Unflatten by the side of your sticker, edit it and then click flatten again.

You can make multiple copies of your sticker by clicking the Duplicate button.

Now is the time to drop your sticker from the screen. Click the Make It Button in the top right corner of your screen to show a preview of how your sticker will look like when you print it. The essence of the preview is to check that the sticker you designed, satisfy you.

Click Continue and select Cricut Explore Air from the dropdown menu and then send it for printing.

Select your desired material from the list of materials by clicking Browse All Materials.

You can try your hands on a number of different designs by playing with the different shapes and edit tools in the Design Space. It is super exciting to see what you will achieve with this experience

Fruity Tray

Materials:

- An octagonal tray, crealia coral, light yellow, white, and leaf green decorative paints.
- One or two flat brushes
- A pencil
- A 10cm paper disc and brown
- Black and glitter green poscas
- Polish glue to varnish spray and masking tape.

Instructions:

1. Draw disks on your board and paint them green (mix leaf green with light yellow) it will be necessary to make 2 layers. After drying, make yellow ovals in the center (light yellow and white) and paint in two coats too. All this can be done using a Cricut template

2. Trace the outlines of the discs in brown. Draw the green lines (see photo) in the green area and then the pips. Apply a spray varnish to prevent the posca from drooling in the glue varnish in the next step.

3. Stick the stickers with the varnish glue at the bottom of the tray. After drying, apply a little varnish in spray to prevent the ink of the stickers from dissolving in contact with the resin.

4. Using a glue gun, attach the small wooden fruit decorations.

Here are some indications for a successful resin.

- First of all, the bottom of the tray must be varnished to prevent inks/colors/paints from bleeding into the paint. It is not systematic, but it could happen, so you better take the lead.

- Then, respect the dosages of the packaging and check that you pour the hardener first. - Mix for a long time. 10 minutes minimum per cup. Here there are two cups I have mixed over 20 minutes. Don't hesitate to transfer your mixture to a new cup and mix again. - pour the resin in the center of the tray and distribute the whole by tilting it.

- Let dry for two days, even if the packaging says 24h.

Craft Paper Pencil Holder

Discover the braiding of strips of craft paper and make a pencil holder in natural colors for your office.

Materials:

- Imitation leather craft paper braiding tape - 9.5 cm
- Self-healing cutting mat - 60x45 cm
- Transparent ruler for creative hobbies 40 cm
- Scissors
- Mini high-temperature glue gun
- Pencil
- Salvaged cardboard, glass, and jar or compass

Instructions:

1. Take a glass and a jar with different diameters. Trace the outlines of the circles on recycled cardboard. Cut with a cutter. In addition to this, you need to know more about it.

2. Glue the cardboard discs together with the glue gun. Cut strips of craft paper braiding 20 cm long. Glue them one by one in radiation. Superimpose them slightly at the base: the bands must be edge to edge at the circumference of the cardboard disc. In addition to this, you need to know more about it.

3. Cover the larger cardboard disc in this way. Glue with a glue gun. Fold the braiding strips, then measure the circumference of the cardboard disc and cut 5 braiding strips of this size. In addition to this, you need to know more about it.

4. Slide a strip of braiding perpendicular under one of those welded to the cardboard base. Stick one end to it, as close as possible to the base. Pass it alternately under one vertical strip and over the next one. Attach a dot of glue to the glue gun under a few vertical strips.

5. To close, glue the second end of the strip under the first end. In the same way, slip the second strip of braiding, mount a second row, tightening to avoid gaping spaces.

6. Set up the braiding of the pot with 5 strips in all. Fold a base strip towards the inside of the pot. Mark the fold in the pot to mark the length. Cut off the excess. In addition to this, you need to know more about it.

7. Cut a strip of braiding a little larger than the circumference of the pot. Glue to the top edge of the pot with a glue gun. Fold the strips one by one towards the inside of the pot. Glue them with a glue gun. R with a glue gun.9. The pot is ready to accommodate the pencils in your office.

Birth Announcement Card

Make an announcement using different Parisian ties to celebrate the birth of your child.

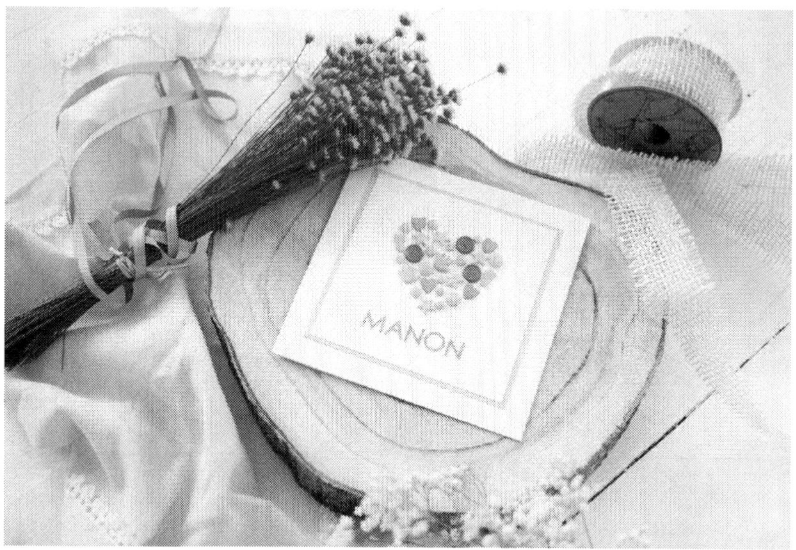

Materials

- Assortment of Parisian ties "newborn girl"
- Assortment of 80 Parisian ties - Pink
- Alphabet Glitter uppercase - Pink
- 25 Pollen folded cards 135x135 mm - White
- Mahé sheet 30.5 x 30.5 cm white
- Mahé sheet 30.5 x 30.5 cm pale pink
- Tube of universal gel glue - Cultura - 30 ml

- Precision cutter and 3 blades
- Self-healing cutting mat - 30x22 cm
- Assortment of 3 precision tools
- Transparent ruler for creative hobbies 30 cm
- Template to download and print

Instructions:

- To start, download, print, and reproduce the heart template. Hollow out the pattern using the cutter to create a stencil.
- Cut an 11 x 11 cm pink square and a 10.5 x 10.5 cm white square.
- Center the stencil on the square of white paper and secure it with adhesive paper to prevent it from moving.
- Place a few Parisian ties to guide you in their positioning inside the cutout heart.
- Using a precision cutter or paper punch, pierce your card and insert the Parisian clips.
- Once the heart is filled, glue the white part on the rose.
- Finish by pasting the desired text (first name...) to finalize the card.
- The invitation is ready.

Cloud Shelf

Decorate this shelf cloud beautiful papers to Koala reasons for decorating children's room very soft.

Materials:

- Créalia "Clouds" wooden shelf
- Acrylic tube 120 matt white
- Flat synthetic brush n ° 18
- Straight scissors - 17 cm
- Transparent ruler for creative hobbies 30 cm
- Precision cutter and 3 blades
- Self-healing cutting mat - 45x35 cm
- Cardboard stickers - Little baby
- Extra strong double-sided adhesive tape - 6mm x 10m

Instructions:

- Paint the cloud shelf white. Let dry.
- Download and transfer the templates to different papers from the collection and compose the decoration.
- Glue the cut papers on the cloud shelf using the extra-strong double-sided tape.
- Personalize the shelf with stickers from the collection.
- Tip: the 30 x 30 cm block of paper offers visuals to frame to decorate your child's room or make scrapbooking albums.
- The cloud shelf is ready to decorate your child's room

DIY Bookmark Cat-Page

Here is the cat-page bookmark, your summer companion!

Materials:

- block of 20 multi-colored postcards sheets
- Glue
- Pouch of 24 decorated colored pencils
- 6 round movable eyes Ø 12mm
- PERFO ROUND CLAMP 6MM
- 5m roll of Glitter masking tape - Green
- 5m roll of Glitter masking tape - White

Instructions:

1. Print the template and choose its paper colors.

2. Cut out the template along the lines.

3. Copy the drawing of the body, front legs, and back legs on the brown sheet, do the same in the purple sheet for the belly, and cut out.

4. Glue the elements together with glue.

   ** To facilitate the gluing put some glue on a cardboard plate and use a brush to spread the glue well. Then clean the brush with warm water and soap.

5. Glue the movable eyes, glue a piece of masking tape to make the collar, cut a piece of pink paper in a triangle for the nose, and with a black pencil draw the mouth, mustaches, and legs.

6. With the hole punch, make a small circle in the yellow paper and glue it to finalize the cat's collar.

** To get an easy triangle nose, first cut out a square and cut it in half diagonally.

7. Write your name on the cat's belly with a colored pencil.

8. And there you have a nice cat-page bookmark for your summer readings. I'm going to reread the adventures of the little wizard, and what will you read?

You can even do it in other colors so you don't get bored!

Table Decoration

Create a fresh and summery decoration for a tropical atmosphere, both on your walls and on your tables! Ideal for your summer evenings to share without moderation!

Materials:

- Set of 6 Scrapbooking paper sheets - Tropical Paradise
- Mahé Leaf - 30.5x30.5cm - petrol blue
- Mahé Leaf - 30.5x30.5cm - menthol green
- Mahé Leaf - 30.5x30.5cm - lime green
- Mahé Leaf - 30.5x30.5cm - spring green
- Slate scrapbooking sheet - Mahé - 30x30cm

- Sheet of 34 epoxy stickers - Tropical Paradise
- 8 card stock polaroid frames - Tropical Paradise
- Assortment of 40 die-cuts - Tropical Paradise
- 100m two-tone spool - Sky blue
- 16 mini clothespins 35 mm
- Vivaldi smooth sheet A4 240g - Canson - white n ° 1
- Precision cutter and 3 blades
- Blue cutting mat - 2mm - A3
- Black acrylic and aluminum ruler 30cm
- Precision scissors 13.5cm blue bi-material rings
- 3D adhesive squares
- Mahé Tools - Easy Mounter - scrapbooking
- Pack of 6 HB graphite pencils

Instructions:

1. Gather the materials.
2. Using the template and a pencil, reproduce the palm tree on the papers in the collection.
3. Download and print the template here.
4. Cut out with a cutter or scissors.

5. Assemble the trunk of the palm tree. Glue the foliage. Using the template, reproduce the traces of the cocktail support on thin cardboard, following the dimensions indicated. Cover it with the collection paper.

6. Download and print the template here.

7. After having cut in the slate sheet: 1 x (8.5 x 8.5 cm). Choose a Polaroid. Glue the slate sheet to the back of the Polaroid. Using a chalk pen, write "Cocktail of the day." Decorate with the stickers. Fold the support at the dotted lines.

8. Using the templates and a pencil, draw the leaves and flowers on the Mahé paper and on the collection paper. Draw.

9. Download and print the leaf and flower template.

10. Choose photos. Cut them to size: 8.5 x 8.5 cm. Stick to the back of the Polaroids.

11. Glue the leaves and flowers together. Cut the string to the desired dimensions and glue it to the back of the flowers. Glue the birds on the string and hang the photos using mini clips.

And here is a pretty summer and tropical decoration! Beautiful evenings in perspective!

Clothespin Card

Materials:

- Clothespin
- Glue
- Painting
- Color paper or illustrations to download
- Decorations: eyes, sequins

Instructions:

1. Start by painting your clothespins.
2. Cut out the illustrations or your colored paper in a heart shape.
3. Come and cut your shape in half in the middle.
4. Apply glue to the ends of your clothespin.

5. And stick your heart or your butterfly on your clothespin.

6. We now add glue to the back of your clothespin to be able to place the small text "I love you."

7. You can also add small decorations to customize your clothespin further. Your laundry card is ready!

Easter Special Containment

It's time to collect at home..... Rolls of toilet paper, colored sheets, markers, and glue

Instructions

1. Cut the height measurements from your roll and glue by wrapping this paper around.
2. With white glue or whatever you have at home.
3. Hold the paper with pins so that it sticks.
4. Then make a template to make ears that we transfer to a paper and that we cut.
5. With another paper, cut out the inside of the ears and glue them.
6. Now, we have to make the eyes.... either you have moving eyes, or you do them yourself like me... For that, we make circles by hand or with perforators.
7. Glue the eyes and ears.
8. Make bunny paws, cut them, and glue them.
9. Draw the nose and whiskers with a felt tip pen.
10. Now we're going to make the paper chick ...
11. Cut 2 rectangles in the paper here 6x14 and 6x12
12. Staple the papers together to make rolls. And superimpose them as below.
13. Cut out beaks and eyes, then glue them.
14. Cut out some feet, glue them, and your chicks are ready!!!

Boat Garland

Here is a garland on the Marine theme to navigate according to our creativity.

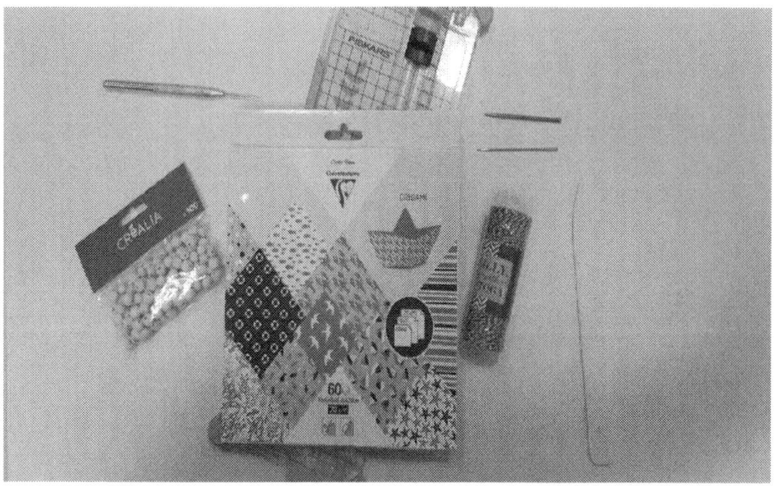

Materials:

- Marine origami papers 70 g / m², Clairefontaine
- 8mm wooden beads, Créalia
- Two-tone blue and white twine, Toga
- A folder
- A paper piercer
- A needle with a large eye
- A cutter
- A pair of scissors

Instructions:

1. Cut the origami papers of different sizes, you need:
    - of 7cm x 10cm
    - 3 of 10.5cm x 15cm
    - 3 of 14cm x 20cm
2. Fold the different squares as shown in the small boat construction diagram below. At each step, remember to use a folder to facilitate folding and not to tear the paper
3. Using the paper punch, pierce the small boats at their tops.
4. Cut 1m of two-colored string. Make a loop 50cm from the wire so that it is in the middle.
5. Using the needle, thread alternately a bead and then a small boat (from the smallest to the largest). Each element must be blocked with a small double knot. Finish with a double knot below the last boat and cut the excess thread that protrudes.
6. All you have to do is hang your garland!

Cutting Letters and Shapes for Scrapbooking

Shapes are one of the most vital features in Cricut Design Space. They are used for creating some of the best designs. In this tutorial, you will learn how to cut letters or texts, how to add shapes, and how to adjust the size, colors, and rotate shapes.

To add a shape;

1. Log into your Design Space.
2. From the drop-down menu, click "Canvas." You will be taken to the canvas or work area.
3. Click "Shapes" on the left panel of the canvas.
4. A window will pop-up with all the shapes available in Cricut Design Space.
5. Click to add shape.

We have explained the process of adding a shape. To cut a shape;

1. Click "Linetype." Linetype lets your machine know whether you plan on cutting, drawing, or scoring a shape.
2. Select "Cut" as Linetype and proceed with cutting the shape.

Cutting Letters

Cutting letters or texts is simple if you know how to do it. To cut letters;

1. First of all, you need to add the text you want to cut. Click "Add Text" on the left panel of the canvas.
2. Place text in the area where you want to cut it. Highlight text and click on the slice tool. If you have multiple lines of text, weld them, and create a single layer. Then use the slice tool.
3. Move the sliced letters from the circle and delete the ones you don't need.

How to Make Simple Handmade Cards

If you want to test your crafting skills, the Cricut Explore Air 2 has made it possible for you to be creative with designing whatever you want to design on the Design Space. We will be teaching you how to use your Cricut Explore Air 2 to make simple cards.

1. Log into Design Space with your details. Do this on your Mac/Windows PC.

2. On the left-hand side of the screen, select "Shapes." Add the square shape.

3. By default, there is no rectangular shape, so you have to make do with the square shape. However, you can adjust the length and width. You can change the shape by clicking on the padlock icon at the bottom left of the screen. Change the size and click on the padlock icon to relock it.

4. Click “Score Line” and align.

5. Create your first line. It's advisable you make it long. Use the "zoom in" option for better seeing if you are having difficulties with sight.

6. Select the first line you have created and duplicate. It's easier that way than creating another long line. You will see the duplicate option when you right-click on your first line.

7. Follow the same duplication process and create a third line.

8. Rotate the third line to the bottom so that it connects the other two parallel lines you earlier created. Remember to zoom in to confirm that the lines are touching.

9. Duplicate another line, just like you did the other. Rotate it to the top so that it touches the two vertical parallel lines. You should have created a big rectangular shape.

10. Highlight your rectangular shape (card). Select "Group" at the upper right corner.

11. Now, change the "Score" option "cut." You can do this by clicking on the little pen icon.

12. Your lines will change from dotted to thick straight lines.

13. Select the "Attach" option at the bottom right-hand side of the screen. The four lines will be attached and will get the card ready to be cut on the mat correctly.

14. You can adjust the size of the card as you like. At this point, you can add images or texts to beautify your card anyhow you want it.

15. After you are done, select the "Make it" button and then "Continue" to cut your card out.

If you don't know how to create a style on your cards with shapes, follow these simple steps to create one.

1. Select your choice of shape. Let's choose stars, for example. Select the "Shape" option and click on the star.

2. Add two stars.

3. Select the first star and click "Flip," and then select "Flip Vertical."

4. Align both stars to overlap them at the center.

5. Select "Weld" to make a new shape and add a score line.

6. Align them at the center and attach them.

7. Select the "Make it button" and then "Continue" to cut your card out.

If you don't know how to add text or write on a card, follow the processes below.

1. Select your choice of shape. Let's choose a hexagon, for example. Select the "Shape" option and click on the hexagon shape.

2. Use your favorite pattern.

3. Add a scoring line and rotate it.

4. Click "Add Text." A box will appear on the canvas or work area of your project. Write your desired text. Let's say you choose to write "A Star Is Born Strong" and "And Rugged" on the two hexagonal shapes. Choose the fonts and style of writing.

5. Select the first text and flip vertically or horizontally.

6. Select the second text and flip vertically. Click "Flip" and select flip vertically. Doing this will make the text not look upside down.

7. Attach Select "Make it button" and then "Continue" to cut your card out. Follow the cutting process on the screen to full effect.

Making a Vinyl Sticker

First of all, you need to have an idea of the vinyl sticker that you want. Get ideas online or from forums. Once you have gotten the picture, make a sketch to see how the sticker would look. After you have done this, follow the steps below;

1. Use an image editing software like Photoshop or Illustrator. Design to your taste and save. Make sure you know the folder it is saved to.
2. Now, open your Design Space.
3. Click "New Project."
4. Scroll to the bottom left-hand side and click "Upload."
5. Drag and drop the design you created with your photo editing app.
6. Select your image type. If you want to keep your design simple, select simple.
7. Select which area of the image is not part of it.
8. Before you forge ahead, select the image as cut to have a preview. You can go back if there is a need for adjustments.
9. Select "Cut."
10. Weed excess vinyl.
11. Use a transfer tape on top of the vinyl. This will make the vinyl stay in position.
12. Go over the tape and ensure all the bibles are nowhere to be found.
13. Peel away the transfer tape, and you have your vinyl sticker.

CHAPTER 3:

Making Money with Cricut

Here are some questions to ask yourself before starting out. Doing an exercise like this will help you streamline your goals and ease your way forward. Ask yourself the following questions:

- Why do you want to sell your crafts? Write down three to four reasons.
- Is this going to be something you want to do part-time, or are you considering making it become your main revenue stream?
- If it is not going to be full-time, do you have enough time to spend on crafting to sustain the business and meet customer demands?
- How well-versed are you in marketing?
- Are you capable of handling the technology side of the business?
- Where would you set up your craft workshop?
- Could you picture yourself crafting day in and day out?
- How well do you deal with difficult people?
- Are you prepared to deal with people from all walks of life?
- Do you have the support to help back you up?

These are tough questions, but a lot of small businesses fail because they weren't able to answer them ahead of time. You need to have a clear, concise plan and vision from the beginning, and you must be sure that this is what you truly want to do. Understanding the why, how, and when is the most important building block for a strong foundational base for any start-up.

There are many things you have to think about before starting your own crafting business. There are copyright issues, licensing concerns, and finding out the limitations on selling your goods, among other considerations.

Before starting out, you should find someone who is business savvy and pick their brain. What first steps do they recommend for you? What pitfalls can they help you avoid? Do the research and learn the A-Z of starting your crafting business to make sure all your I's and T's are dotted and crossed.

50+ Business Ideas You Can Make With Your Cricut and Sell

- Wall art canvas
- Leather bracelet
- Frosty wreath,
- Iron-on T-shirt
- Customized tools
- Customized cutting board
- Customized kitchen towels

- Customized lanyards
- Doormats
- Rustic signs
- Coffee mugs
- Holiday bucket
- Customized plates
- Pillows case
- Bed sheets
- Paper succulent
- Planner stickers
- Sports cuff
- Key chains
- Wooden signs
- Monogrammed ornament
- Blankets
- Laptop cases
- Monogrammed pillows
- Car stickers

- Home decals
- Christmas greeting cards
- Interior designs
- Pet tags
- Cake tops
- Scrapbook pages
- Gift boxes
- Addressed envelopes
- Felt coasters
- Customized tote bags
- Flower bouquets
- Monogrammed water bottle
- Model decals
- Paper pennants
- Metallic tags
- Paper peonies
- Santa sacks
- Christmas advent calendar

- Paper heart box
- Paper tulips
- Magnolia blossom
- Gift card holder
- Paper flower lanterns
- Paper purse
- Paper poppers
- Halloween buddies
- Paper fiery house and more

How to Save Money While Using Your Cricut Explore Machine for Business

For beginners, this is the part that gives them the most headaches, especially when your pocket is not friendly to accommodate your supplies for project and craft. So, I want to help you suggest ways you can make the most use of your Cricut Explore machine for business and get your supplies at the cheapest prices. You don't have to be fleeced of your hard-earned money any longer. The first thing is to read the instructions on how to use your Cricut Explore machine properly. It is not for fun that manufacturers place instruction guides for their products. It is meant to help you get the most out of your machine. Follow the instructions carefully, and you will save yourself some extra cash that would have been used for repairs and new purchases. You will replace your cutting mat, depending on the usage, from time to time. Try to make use of the 12" x 24" mat because the long mats save you a lot of money. You can turn to the other side when the adhesive strength of the first side begins to diminish. Instead of buying another one, just flip it over and continue with your next project.

The blades can drain your pocket when you don't make the most use of it. I don't need to tell you about the importance of a sharp blade when cutting. If you must save money, take proper care of your blades, organize them, and never misuse the blade to cut inappropriate materials. Anything contrary to that means you will be replacing your blade often, which is money draining from your pocket. For your vinyl products, I suggest you use Expressions Vinyl, which is cheaper than the other vinyl materials and even give the same feel to your project.

Best Piece of Vinyl to Use for Your Projects: Business and Personal Adhesive Vinyl

Different vinyl manufacturers are churning out different products for craft, different colors, textures, and options. Be careful what piece of vinyl material you use for your project so that you don't ruin your project. Know the different types if you must work with the vinyl material or use the recommended one for your project.

Adhesive Vinyl

This is the most common vinyl material on the market. You will come across it regularly in your starter kit with your machine. It comes attached to a carrier sheet coated with silicone, and you can easily pull the vinyl off. Use transfer tape to transfer it to its final place on your project, that is, after it has been cut and weeded. There are two types of adhesive vinyl materials: removable and permanent. Removable adhesive vinyl is the regular Cricut vinyl material mostly used for indoors, temporal outdoor event, or placed on any surface that will not touch regularly or in need of a wash (wall decal). If I suggest it, I will go for Oracal 631. On the other hand, permanent adhesive vinyl is waterproof and lasts longer than temporal adhesive vinyl.

They are usually rated to last six years or more. Its application is in DIY projects that need to be washed regularly such as tumblers, shot glasses, exterior walls, car decals, and more.

Heat Transfer Vinyl

This is the type used for fabrics. It is designed to bond to the fabric when heat and pressure are applied to it. Some features can help you determine the best quality of heat transfer vinyl material: color, finish, ease of weeding, price, durability, and cut reliability. Unlike adhesive vinyl, heat transfer vinyl does not require transfer tape. I will suggest Siser EasyWeed Heat Transfer Vinyl as the best of the rest.

Cling Vinyl

This is a type of vinyl material with no adhesive attached to it but uses static electricity to attach to smooth surfaces like window panes and removable decorations on mirrors. It can be removed and reused again on dry and clean surfaces. I will suggest Grafix Cling Vinyl Film to you.

Ideas for Selling Your Cricut Crafts

The following ideas assume that you have the full legal rights to sell all the crafts you are making.

- First, narrow down your product niche. Find a few products that you enjoy creating and that there is a demand for.
- Be creative and unique. Make your own niche or start a new trend. You want there to be a market for your product, but not one that's already oversaturated.
- Don't shy away from festivals or markets. Find out when and where there are events in or around your area. Get yourself out there. Ask your friends and family to come with you.

- Make flyers! Yes, people do still use flyers, especially at large events. You need to draw people's attention to you. Flyers can be annoying, but they also get a person's attention.

- Give small samples of your products out. If people like them, they'll be encouraged to come back for more, this time with their wallets ready.

- Ask family and friends to use your products. There is no quicker way to catch a person's eye than when someone else has something they don't or is using it regularly. Family and friends are great promoters, and since they are by your side, they can be your staunchest supporters. They can also give you positive reviews and testimonials online.

- Build a website. There are many easy to use websites such as Wix, Squarespace, Moonfruit, and more. They have hundreds of already-made templates that you can easily customize to suit your needs. You can even start a crafting blog with tips, tricks, and project instructions to pull more people in.

- Use social media to your advantage. Facebook, Twitter, Instagram, and all the other social media platforms out there can help get your products seen by potentially millions of customers.

- There is no harm in approaching small shops that sell arts and crafts to ask them to take some consignment stock.

- Make your gifts for baby showers, birthdays, holidays, and even weddings.

- You can rent small stalls in large shopping malls. These stalls are usually in the middle of busy walkways.

These are some of the ways to get your crafts out there and make money selling customized homemade goods. What you have to remember when you do start selling your crafts is that it may not take off right away. Most of the successful businesses out there today had slow or rocky starts. You can't give up on your first try. If you are serious about making money with your crafts, you have to push through the hard times to get to the good ones.

Online Marketplaces for Selling Crafts

The websites that you will find below are probably already familiar to you, even by hearsay, because they are the most popular in the craft world.

All allow you to create your store within it, with your name, logo, and description; display your items, serve your customers, and manage orders and payments. So they work in much the same way. As I anticipated, Etsy is the most famous globally, and especially in the United States. DaWanda stands out particularly in Europe, with a large influx of German public. I will tell you in a little more detail.

Etsy

Buy what you can think of creative people from all over the world

Etsy is an American platform that has been growing in popularity since it was created to become the number 1 marketplace to sell handmade worldwide. Here you can sell all kinds of handmade products, as well as vintage and even DIY materials and patterns. Besides, you can find forums and discussion groups with a lot of activities in which to connect with like-minded people. Most are in English. Fortunately, not all. Due to the huge volume of traffic that this platform has every day, especially from the United States, it is one of the marketplaces preferred by many artisans to start. Opening a store is easier than it may seem a priori, especially if you follow some tutorial that explains step by step and in great detail how you can open your store on Etsy.

Creating your own shop on Etsy will cost you nothing. What you will have to pay is a publication fee of 20 cents for each item you put up for sale in your store, in addition to a 3.5% commission for each transaction.

Artesanum

The world's arts and crafts store Artesanum is a platform that was created to become the largest online market for the sale of arts and crafts in Spanish. Something that I value very positively is that it was founded in 2007 as a social project of the Intercom Group, and it donates the profits generated by Artesanum to projects related to crafts. Also, artisans agree that it is very easy to use. Something that differentiates it from other marketplaces is that purchases are made directly from the artisan, so the customer buys and pays at each Artesanum store independently (this means that they do not collect items from different stores in a cart).

Who creates a store in Artesanum has two possibilities:

- Use your store as a showcase to list your crafts and contact potential buyers by courier for free.
- Add payment tools to the store in exchange for 5% for each sale.

As I mentioned at the beginning, my intention with this compilation is to offer you a lot of possibilities to sell your crafts online with little investment so that you can choose the ones that suit you best. That bunch of options certainly includes more marketplaces. The online marketplaces below may not be that popular, but… who knows. Perhaps among them, you discover the perfect option for you.

Lulishop

Original Mediterranean Products

I had the opportunity to chat with the team that created this marketplace to tell me more about the project and have already published the interview on the blog.

If you have not seen it and you do not know anything about this marketplace, I can tell you that it was created in Corsica with the idea of facilitating the online sale of their crafts to artisans in that region and due to the success achieved it has been extended to focus on the sale of Mediterranean crafts today.

Coolmaison

Coolmaison is an online craft store specializing in handmade jewelry, tableware, and decoration, which stands out for its designs' exclusivity and quality.

It is a platform that is committed to avant-garde craftsmanship, so not just any handmade piece is worth being there.

Artisans who want to sell with them must send their application and go through a selection process.

Once inside, you will have a dashboard where you can find all the information, promotional tools, and statistics.

When you have orders and messages from clients, they will inform you by e-mail.

If you are targeting an audience that buys designer handmade,

Coolmaison could be the perfect option for you

Unique Species

Buy and give crafts and unique products

Unique Species is an online store that sells handmade items that are characterized by their design, uniqueness, and sustainability.

This makes them very selective with the products that are sold since they seek to guarantee their customers their quality and sustainability.

They are in charge of all the management and promotion of the items in the store. You will only have to worry about sending the order when they contact you to communicate that there has been a sale.

Like other platforms of the style, it works on commission. And they are open to working with new professionals like you

If you think that your creations could fit into that concept of "unique species" and you want to become one of the partners of this online store, go ahead and contact them.

Manos Es Más

It is another famous marketplace that sells quality, exclusive and trendy pieces of Spanish crafts.

It only accepts artisans with trade resident in Spain. For this reason, the team carries out a strict selection of new stores, validating each of the announcements of the articles uploaded to it before its publication.

Putting your crafts for sale will not cost you anything, since Manos es más does not charge you for creating the store or for publishing your articles.

They will take a commission of 4% of your sales.

ArtesOs

Online Market of Crafts, Sustainable Fashion and Vintage.

If you develop your activity with sustainable criteria, your site may be here.

ArtesOs is an online platform for the purchase and sale of crafts and sustainable fashion.

Here you will have the possibility to sell your products for free. ArtesOs will keep 10% of the total price of each sale, not including shipping costs.

Of course, you must have a PayPal account, because you will need it to receive your sales made through this marketplace.

Artenet

Artenet is an online platform to directly buy paintings and original art from artists around the world that has a section dedicated exclusively to crafts.

This website works more as a showcase to display your works than as a store because Artenet does not get involved in transactions or manage payments.

Whoever is interested in buying your pieces can contact you directly, and together you will agree on how to make the payment and shipping of the work.

The good news is that signing up for Artenet is free, publishing your creations as well, and it also doesn't charge a sales commission.

Artmosfair

The fair trade art market.

Artmosfair is an online fair trade marketplace where you can buy and sell exclusive handmade art. An art that can range from the craftsmanship created by an older woman to the art of the Da Vinci level.

Although this marketplace is focused on Europe, it has a place for painting, crafts, and sculpture of all cultures. For Artmosfair, "Nothing is too small or too exclusive."

They charge a small commission for the publication of articles and a percentage of the sale amount in each transaction that varies depending on the chosen plan.

They offer two possibilities:

- The Basic plan, which is great to start with. They will charge you €0.10 per published article, and you can sell your first 6 articles without commission. Then a sales commission of 6% will be applied to you.

- The Plus plan, for when the Basic plan falls short. You can publish your articles at no cost, and the sales commission that will be applied in this case will be 3%. In addition, you will have the possibility to upload your articles to the first positions in the search results at no cost.

There are some websites specialized in the purchase and sale of crafts that work all over the world and allow any crafter, regardless of where they are, to open their store. There is only one catch: they are not available in Spanish.

The limitation of the language can be an inconvenience for many people, but if it is not your case and you can handle yourself perfectly in English (and you are addressing an audience that also speaks the language, of course), these platforms are a more than interesting option to consider.

Waremakers

Waremakers is a Danish company, also based in Valencia, which distinguishes itself from other platforms in the artisanal sector due to its specialization in the sale of top quality handmade items. They seek excellence.

If you want to sell your crafts in this online store, you can write to them on their website.

Waremakers will contact you to see what type of articles among those you produce to fit the profile they are looking for.

If you reach an agreement, the Waremakers team will take care of everything: create your store, manage the products for you, promote your products ... The only thing you have to do is set a price and send the items that are sold to the address that they indicate.

Opening and maintaining your store will cost you nothing. They will only take a commission for each item sold.

Artfire

Premier handmade marketplace to buy & sell handmade.

ArtFire is a platform for selling handmade, vintage, and DIY items online, which was created by American artisans for artisans around the world.

It puts at your disposal some tools to promote your products, as well as a support team available via chat and a community.

You can choose between different plans when it comes to selling with them. For the most popular you will have to pay $20 per month and a 3% commission for each item sold.

Zibbet

Buy unique handmade products, fine art, vintage, and craft.

Zibbet is a marketplace for independent creatives that allows you to create your own independent store, with its own domain, in addition to the one on its platform.

From the control panel, you can manage both your store in the marketplace and your website and analyze your statistics.

Also, if you already sell on Etsy you can import your items from there and save yourself the trouble of uploading all the products again.

Unlike most marketplaces, Zibbet will not charge you transaction fees or fees for listing your products. You will have to pay a monthly fee that varies depending on the plan and the chosen payment method, from $4 to $20 per month.

Those marketplaces with a greater number of buyers around the world have also echoed the boom that handmade products are experiencing in recent times.

We are not all equal. We don't all want to wear the same clothes that everyone else wears. Nor decorate the house in the same way. Nor do we have the same ideas.

We are different, and more and more people are seeking to express their individuality, their values , and their philosophy of life through their purchases.

This trend has not gone unnoticed by platforms such as Amazon or eBay, which have created the Crafts category to get closer to these types of customers while giving small artisan shops the possibility of being visible by millions of people throughout the world.

However, that also comes at a price. The commissions that are applied per transaction in these marketplaces are somewhat higher than those of the rest.

And also take into account the competition that you are going to face within the same marketplace, which also sells products that have not been made by hand.

At least Amazon filters out the artisans who become part of its Handmade community. On eBay, on the other hand, they sell a little bit of everything within the categories where the crafts are found, from materials to creations that do not really know where they come from or who has made them.

That is why I am not going to go into more detail about selling crafts on eBay. It is possible to do so, but I would not consider this option. Whoever enters eBay I don't think they are very aware of the value of what you are offering.

Amazon Handmade

If you create your store on Amazon Handmade you can sell your items on Amazon's five European platforms: Amazon.co.uk, Amazon.de, Amazon.fr, Amazon.it and Amazon.com

For this, you will have to request an invitation. The Amazon Handmade team will study your request to see if you meet the requirements of their definition of "handmade," and if you meet it, they will send you an invitation to enter and set up your store.

Afterward, you will be charged a commission per sale that will no longer be promotional, but the standard reference commission, which will vary depending on the category your products are in (you can see the list here). It seems that also, from that date, December 31, they could charge you a monthly fee.

With this plan, you can witness one of the great disadvantages of selling on Amazon (and in any marketplace for that matter): you accept its conditions, and they can change at any time. You are not in control. You are giving it to others.

If you want to have control over your own business, have at least your own website, and attract your own customers.

Conclusion

Cricut machines are awesome gadgets to own because they do not only boost creativity and productivity, they can also be used to create crafts for business. With Design Space, crafters can create almost anything and even customize their products to bear their imprints.

All over the world, people use these machines to make gift items, T-shirts, interior décor, and many other crafts, to beautify their homes, share with friends and family during holidays, and even sell, etc.

There two types of Cricut machines; the Cricut Explore and the Cricut Maker. Both machines are highly efficient in their rights, and experts in the crafting world make use of them to create a plethora of items, either as a hobby or for business.

Both machines are similar in many ways, i.e., the Cricut Maker and the Explore Air 2, but the Cricut Maker is somewhat of a more advanced machine because it comes with some advanced features, as compared to the Explore Air 2.

One distinct feature about the Maker that sets it apart from the Explore Air is the fact that it can cut thicker materials. With the Maker, the possibilities are limitless, and crafters can embark on projects that were never possible with Cricut machines before the release of the Make.

Another feature that puts the Cricut Maker machine ahead of the Explore Air 2 is the 'Adaptive Tool System.' With this tool, the Cricut Maker has been empowered in such a way that it will remain relevant for many years to come because it will be compatible with new blades and other accessories that Cricut will release in the foreseeable future.

Although both machines have several dissimilarities, there are also areas where they completely inseparable. Let's take for example the designing of projects in Cricut Design Space.

Cricut Design Space is the software where all the magnificent designs are made before they are sent to be cut. It is one of the most important aspects in the creation of crafts in the Cricut set up. However, when it comes to Cricut Maker and the Explore Air 2, there is nothing to separate them in this regard, because both machines use the same software for project design.

As a crafter, without proper knowledge of Design Space, you're not only going to cut out poor products, you will also make little or no in-road in your quest to find success.

Understanding Design Space is important because it empowers crafters with enormous tools and materials to create generalized and custom products. It is an extremely powerful tool that just cannot be overlooked by anyone that intends to follow this path.

Thus, the understanding of Design Space is a MUST for people that intend to make a business out of Cricut machines or even utilize it as a hobby. With the software, crafters can create their designs from scratch or use already-made designs on the Cricut platform. Those that have an active subscription to Cricut Access have access to thousands of images, projects, and fonts. They can cut out their products using these images or projects, and they can also edit them to suit their style and taste before cutting.

Cricut Design Space comes with some exciting tools and features that can make crafting easy and straightforward. These tools are not so hard to use, so to get conversant with them, you need to do some research and consistently apply the knowledge you gain from your research and reading. Expert crafters know all about the important tools in Cricut Design Space, as well as the role they play in the design of projects.

Some of these tools include; the slice tool, weld tool, contour tool, attach tool and flatten tool, etc.

Cricut machines do not function separately -when you purchase them, they come with accessories and tools that are required for them to function. Minus the tools and accessories that come in the pack, others can be purchased separately to boost the machine's functionality and output.

In terms of the Cricut Design Space software and app, some tips and tricks aid the process of project design and production. The software is easy and straightforward to learn and design on, but like any other application and software, it still has some related issues and problems.

When problems arise, solutions are naturally proffered, and in terms of Cricut Design Space, there are several ways to address app-related issues to improve user experience and functionality. This book covers several solutions to the issues related to the Design Space app and software.

The Design Space software is web-based, so some laptop computers are perfectly suited for the purpose. These laptops are suitable for several reasons, including; speed, Space and design, etc. In summary, the best five are; Asus Vivobook F510UA, Dell Inspiron 15 5575, Lenovo Ideapad 330S, Asus Vivobook S410UN, and the Acer Aspire E 15.

Everything on earth needs maintenance, including Cricut machines. These machines are constantly cutting out materials of different textures, shapes, and quantity, etc. Thus, they need routine maintenance to boost their productivity levels and increase their life span.

The routine maintenance of these machines does not require a lot, and as a matter of fact, the hardware needs cleaning after cutting out materials. Thus, non-alcoholic baby wipes are highly recommended for cleaning material residue on the machines. The cutting mat is another item that needs maintenance from time to time because excessive usage without proper care reduces its stickiness.

In terms of projects, there are so many items that can be designed and cut out from Cricut machines.

Also, these items can be sold in the crafts market for profit. Although some people use these machines for recreational purposes, there are even more people who use them for commercial purposes.

Commercial users of Cricut machines design and cut out items to sell for profit, and the machines have proven to be a blast.

One of the reasons why people can sell items made from the Cricut machine is because they have the option of creating custom and unique products that cannot be found anywhere else.

Cricut machines are awesome tools that should be on everybody's radar, especially people that love crafts.